"I cried every night. We may never know the damage we did to these people."

A NURSE *at the Wesley Nursing Home*

. . .

"Wow. Wow. Wow. I just finished your book and I feel like I just spent some time with mom."

TRACY CHEIFETZ, *my sister*

. . .

"I can't think of a more fierce advocate for our business and community than you. Thank you, Todd."

ANTHONY MASTROIANNI, *owner, iRun Local*

. . .

"Anyone that has ever had to deal with the journey of Alzheimer's needs to read this book."

JOHN MARCANTONIO

. . .

A great accomplishment -- and a lasting tribute to your mom and your love, not to mention your leadership through such a dark and difficult time."

KIMBERLY BURGART WEIR

. . .

"Good balance between the very personal and the broader community concerns. And, yes, you made me cry."

BARBARA CAIMANO

I'm Not Ready For This...

...*a memoir by*
Todd Shimkus

I'm Not Ready For This
Copyright © 2023 by Todd Shimkus

All rights reserved. No part of this book may be used or reproduced in any form, electronic or mechanical, including photocopying, recording, or scanning into any information storage and retrieval system, without written permission from the author except in the case of brief quotation embodied in critical articles and reviews.

BOOK DESIGN BY The Troy Book Makers
EDITED BY Katelynne Shimkus

Printed in the United States of America
The Troy Book Makers • Troy, New York • thetroybookmakers.com

To order additional copies of this title, contact your favorite local bookstore or visit www.shoptbmbooks.com

ISBN: 978-1-61468-781-8

"So what are you doing today?" my mom often asked me. Some days, I told her I was writing a book. "What is it about?" she asked on her better days. To which I replied, "It's about you." Then she'd laugh and give me a look that said, "Who would write a book about me?" Well I did because I believe her story needed to be told and mine too.

*"I appoint my son, Todd Shimkus, to serve as my agent.
I was competent when I executed this power of attorney."*

AMY A. SHIMKUS, September 14, 2016

DECEMBER 26, 2019

A TABLE AND TWO CHAIRS sat in the corner just outside the small cafeteria. A painted mural covered the walls on two sides of the table. If you took a photo of my mom and I sitting here with the mural as a backdrop, you might think we were at some fancy outdoor café in Paris. We weren't.

Instead, my mom and I were on the second floor of the Victoria Building on the Wesley Health Care Center campus, in Saratoga Springs, New York. This was my mom's first day here. She was now a resident on 2 Victoria, the Wesley's memory care unit.

I drove her to this facility from my home, one mile away, after we stopped at Kru Coffee. I had what my friends at Kru call "the Todd:" a large skim milk latte. I pick one up there most days on my way to work at the Saratoga County Chamber of Commerce. Today, my mom got her usual as well, a small black coffee with two splendas. We had been to Kru together before. Normally, after we finished our coffee we went back to my house. Today, we drove up the hill in the opposite direction - away from my home, towards the Wesley.

I parked the car as close to the main entrance as possible. The shorter the walk, the less time there'd be for questions. I told my mom to make sure she had her stuffed animal dog, cell phone and purse as she got out of the car. I opened the back hatch and pulled out her suitcase. She had no idea where we were or where she was going.

Just three years ago, in 2016, she appointed me as her agent which empowered me to make all of her health and life decisions. To be an effective caretaker, I asked her to define what was important to her if I needed to make a life or death decision. There were three things she wanted to be able to do if she survived.

"I want to be able to dress and feed myself," she told me. "I want to be able to walk with Ribbie, even if I need a cane or walker. I want to have meaningful conversations with my grandchildren."

When I heard this, I asked, "but what if you won't remember these conversations?" She thought for a moment and replied, "if I can't remember them, what good are they? I don't want to be saved if I can't remember anything."

I was glad we had this conversation but we mistakenly assumed that such a decision would be made after something catastrophic happened. Instead, her mental health declined slowly over many years. Now in 2019, she walked her dog, Ribbie, every day, but she didn't remember this an hour later. Every day she dressed herself, but some days she put on the same clothes from the day before.

Because she trusted me to care for her, today she followed me into the Wesley without hesitation. I will bet that she thought we were taking another one of our adventures; to a great local restaurant, to see the horses at the Saratoga Race Course or the flowers at Yaddo Gardens; or maybe to watch one of her grandchildren perform in a musical or on an athletic field.

I signed us in at the front desk. A nurse was called, and she came to escort us. The three of us got in an elevator, and we went up to the second floor. We were shown to Room 213B and I put my mom's suitcase on the bed.

Everything happened so fast. The nurse took my mom for a walk, while a different staff member handed me several plastic bags. She asked me to put my mom's clothes in these bags so the staff could tag them with her name. This prevented them from getting lost or stolen. Wherever there was shelf space, I put up photos of my mom with her three children, her six grandchildren, and several that featured her with Ribbie.

When my mom and the nurse came back, we made our way out to the hallway and the table in the corner. As we sat here, my mom looked down the short corridor to our right and the long corridor in front of us. Each corridor had older residents that walked around, some on their own and others with walkers. They were mostly women. Some carried stuffed animals like my mom, or baby dolls. The floors were spotless and the hallways bright. The Wesley staff moved in and out of the rooms. Everyone that worked there seemed friendly. They all said hi as they walked past us.

My mom looked directly at me, and her chin quivered as tears filled her eyes. "Todd, I don't belong here. Please, I'm not ready for this," she pleaded. None of us were ready for this. Not her. Not me. Not my younger sisters, Tracy and Trisha. Not my mom's two older sisters, Betty and Joanie.

I put my hand over hers, smiled, bit my tongue, and tried not to tear up myself. "I love you mom. I want you to be safe. We want you to live in Saratoga Springs, close to our home," I told her. "My office is just down the street. I will visit you every single day. You're a Saratogian now - just like Lisa and me."

My mom and I found ourselves at Wesley on December 26, 2019. Normally a day to return holiday gifts you didn't want or clothes that didn't fit. But the day after Christmas, I brought my mom, Amy, to her new home. A nursing home where experts on the memory care unit could really manage her Alzheimer's and keep her safe.

I never told her that she was being taken to a nursing home. My sisters and I didn't involve her in this decision. Tracy consulted with her doctor and she wrote a letter that supported this decision. Even if we talked with our mom, there was no chance she'd remember what was decided, so we just did it to keep her safe.

In this new place for the first time, my mom was traumatized. She had a moment of clarity where she understood exactly what this meant. Later that day, I realized how this change must have seemed abrupt and sudden for her.

Less than 24 hours before, she had so much fun on Christmas Day with all of us. My wife, Lisa, our daughter Katie, my mom and I all wore silly matching Christmas pajamas with llamas on them. We posed with big smiles as we wore them for our annual Christmas photo in front of the tree.

The four of us played table games. One of them was a miniature bowling set. We took turns and tried to roll the ball to knock over the pins. Instead of rolling the ball, my mom bounced it down the length of the table. She missed all of the pins, and we laughed out loud. I want to remember this Christmas bowling moment forever. What I did to my mom right now, just a day later, I did not want to remember as much - it was overwhelmingly sad for both of us.

To add a little insult to injury, December 26 is my wedding anniversary. It was on this very day, twenty seven years ago, in 1992, that Lisa and I were married in the First Congregational Church, in Princeton, Massachusetts. It was Lisa who wanted a Christmas wedding. She loves the decorations, the snow, giving and receiving gifts, and spending this time with family.

Now let's be honest. There is no good day to put your mom in a nursing home. No one ever wants to have to do this. But the day after Christmas? And on my wedding anniversary? My mom was absolutely right. We didn't belong here. Not on this day especially.

But when a parent or someone you love has Alzheimer's, there are a lot of things totally out of your control. We could no longer ensure her safety. She needed help and we did too. No one wanted to wait too long and risk her getting hurt or worse.

When I was a child, my mom was the spectator, not the participant. It was Tracy, Trisha, and me that played sports. When we went on our annual family vacation to Wildwood, New Jersey, it was the three of us that played the games or rode the rides.

My dad, Herb, was an active participant as well. He'd go on all of the rides. He built the sandcastles and taught us to body surf. My mom enjoyed watching us have fun. She was the consummate caregiver, at home and at Holden Hospital where she worked full-time as a registered nurse.

Since her Alzheimer's diagnosis eight years ago, I made every effort to make the moments we spent together fun. Creating these moments was important for me because I knew no one recovered from Alzheimer's. The more moments of pure joy we shared together, the easier I hoped it would be for me to deal with this disease.

One of my favorite moments was when Lisa and I visited her in Virginia. She lived there with Tracy, her husband Craig, and their three kids, Jared, Joel, and Jason. Everyone in my family knows that I love to golf. It was my mother's father, Benny, who taught me how to play. So Tracy arranged for us to go to Top Golf.

Everyone golfed except my mom. I decided to invite her to take a swing. I was relentless and asked over and over again. At one point, Lisa quietly asked me to stop harassing her. I just wanted my mom to try. I planned to coach her, and knew she'd enjoy this moment. If she hit the ball off the platform, it was guaranteed to go in a hole and Grammy Amy would make a hole in one as everyone watched.

My mom finally relented. She stepped up to the tee. I gave her a club, put the ball on the tee and showed her where to stand. "Pretend you are sweeping," I told her. "You just want to bring the club back a little, like you have a broom and sweep the ball off the tee. You can do this."

My mom just needed to make contact between the club and the ball. She didn't need to hit the golf ball hard or even get it in the air. It just needed to roll off the edge. Tracy and her three kids had their cell phones out to record this moment.

My mom moved the club back slowly away from the ball. She swept the club forward and thankfully made contact. The ball bounced off the platform and rolled over the edge. It hit the ground below and rolled slowly until it dropped into a hole.

I held up my right hand and she did the same. We high fived while everyone cheered. "You got a hole in one," I told her. "You took one swing and got a hole in one. That's amazing."

This past summer, I took her on the backstretch at the Saratoga Race Course to the horse stables. We were on this tour with my co-workers at the Saratoga County Chamber. Most were cautious as they approached the horses because they could be a little jumpy. Not my mom. She went right up to the stalls and gently petted them. My mom loved animals, dogs, cats, horses. Being with them comforted her, and they seemed to love her too.

I love that photo of our high five, and I smile when I think of her with the horses. When I think of my mom, those are the moments I want to remember. I did not take photos today of the two of us in the nursing home. As we sat at this table, I listened to her plead with me not to leave her here. She wasn't angry. Rather, she seemed disappointed and scared.

The Christmas Holiday season has almost always been a time of joy and celebration for me and my family, not sadness. Since my two children, Katie and Ben, became adults and moved away to college and then to work, the days between Christmas and New Year's became a convenient time for the four of us to set off on our own adventures.

We went to France in 2013 and spent Christmas Day in Paris, where we visited the Notre Dame Cathedral, the Eiffel Tower, and the Arc de Triomphe. That was when Katie lived in Belgium where she earned a Master's Degree in Literature from the Catholic University of Leuven. Ben, Lisa and I flew over to spend that holiday with her. We explored Paris, Brugge, Ypres, Leuven, and Antwerp. I mistakenly left my cell phone in the car when we got to the airport to leave, so I had no access to calls, text messages, or emails. Lisa, Katie and Ben thought this was a great Christmas gift. I think everyone at the Chamber did too.

Lisa Davis Shimkus is with **Ben Shimkus** and 2 others.
Apr 16, 2019

One of the best days of my life was spent visiting this beautiful Cathedral in Paris. Christmas Day, 2013, spent with my favorite people, visiting Norte Dame and lighting a candle in honor of my mom, in front of the shrine for St. Theresa. What a tremendous loss.

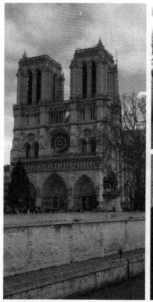

Now in 2019, Ben was a performer on a cruise ship in the Caribbean so a family trip was impossible. He left in September, his contract with the Oceania Riviera ran until the middle of March 2020. He loved to perform on stage, where he sang, danced, tumbled and acted. This Christmas, the only way for us to spend time with Ben was virtually, not in person. We used FaceTime to do so, as we had never heard of Zoom.

Katie now worked at the MIT Press and Bookstore, in Cambridge, Massachusetts. The store needed her for holiday sales and post-holiday returns. Lisa drove to pick up Katie on December 23 and brought her to Saratoga. On December 26, while I took my mom to the Wesley, Lisa drove Katie back to Boston.

My mom and I arrived at the Wesley by 10 a.m. Two hours later, just before lunch, a Wesley staff member came over and took my seat. "Hi Amy, when your son leaves, we can get some lunch together," she said enthusiastically. Taking the cue that it was time for me to go, I told my mom that I had something important to do at work that would make a lot of people happy. Then, I gave my mom a hug and told her I loved her. She said nothing.

I got up and turned to walk toward the elevator and decided not to look back. As I got on the elevator and the doors closed, it helped that I had to immediately refocus my energy and mind on something positive on this otherwise miserable day. In just a few minutes, she ate lunch with strangers while I was in front of television cameras to make a big announcement.

I became the President of the Saratoga County Chamber of Commerce on July 6, 2010, and my first priority was to sustain Saratoga's economic success. In the 1960's, the city fell on hard times. Fortunes faded, and the Chamber was one of the organizations that helped lead a dramatic turn around. As Saratoga's economy was revitalized, the Chamber's resources, capabilities and influence expanded.

The Chamber went from 300 members to more than 2,000 from 1970 until 2019. The Chamber's staff fifty years ago was the President and a part-time assistant. Now we had a team of ten and a $2 million budget. My predecessor, Joe Dalton, is a Marine, a Vietnam Veteran, and a legend in the Chamber world for what he did to revitalize this community and the Chamber over his 40 year tenure.

When Joe retired, those of us who were candidates to replace him all asked ourselves: Is it a good career move to follow a legend like him? At the end of my first interview, I asked the search committee one question: "Everyone knows the amazing work Joe did. But what I'd like to know is what are you looking for in the next President? I want to be sure I have the skills to do what you think is necessary. This must be a good fit for you and me."

One of the members sat up, looked me straight in the eyes, and said; "Joe Dalton is a friend of mine. But we're not looking for another Joe Dalton." He then rattled off priorities he thought the next president should champion. The others chimed in and I suddenly realized this was my dream job.

They wanted someone who was creative, a collaborator, and a great communicator. What they wanted matched what I thought I could do. A few years later, a long-time Chamber volunteer told me: "You had some HUGE shoes to fill when you started, and you filled them well. Your leadership matters more than you know!"

Once called the "Summer Place to Be," Saratoga was now a destination that attracted millions of visitors twelve months of the year. The Saratoga Race Course, the Saratoga Performing Arts Center, and our vibrant downtown with hundreds of unique and locally owned shops and restaurants is a world class destination. Leisure tourists. Business professionals. Conventioneers and exhibitors. Students that attend Skidmore College. Brides and grooms. Retirees and young professionals - all flocked to Saratoga.

In 2019, City officials approved permits for 64 events. Each was designed to attract people to the downtown, and to give them a fun reason to visit and spend money. This included events like ChowderFest, the Firecracker 4 road race on July 4th, the Victorian Streetwalk, and First Night Saratoga.

First Night featured dozens of local artists at more than 40 venues. Thousands of people purchased buttons to attend these shows. At one time, First Night included two fireworks shows: one at 6 p.m. deemed kid-friendly, while a second at midnight was for the adults. This year there were no fireworks.

Mark Mulholland, a reporter with News Channel 13, called me about this. I told Mark that the Arts Council couldn't afford the fireworks. In my interview, I said: "Most people believe the City runs and pays for these events. The reality is the City charges the organizers thousands of dollars to host them. That's why the fireworks are not happening. The City doesn't contribute one dime. But they charge thousands."

The next morning, the Mayor texted me: "I have someone who will pay for the fireworks if you want them." A local fireworks company called and offered me a deal too. Darryl Leggieri, who runs Discover Saratoga; Ryan McMahon, who runs the City Center; and Deann Devitt, the head of the Saratoga Downtown Business Association offered to help. Two years prior, Ryan, Darryl, Deann, and I collaborated to save a different event. Since then, we met regularly to collaborate even more. Joining forces to save the fireworks now was simple compared with the crisis we'd soon face.

The money was easy, but getting a city permit in less than ten days, not so much. That's because our City is one of the few places in the world with a Commission form of government. Here no one person is in charge. We don't have a strong mayor or a City Manager. Instead, we have a Commissioner of Public Safety; a Commissioner of Public Works; a Commissioner of Finance; and a Commissioner of Accounts.

There is also a Mayor, but the powers of this office are limited. The Mayor moderates the meetings of these five elected leaders and oversees the planning and legal departments. Each of these elected positions has a term of just two years and an annual salary of $15,000, which means it's really a thankless job. So when the Mayor texted me to let me know a local developer would pay for the fireworks, she could do little else to help.

The Commission form of government was adopted in 1916, and was modeled after Galveston, Texas. In a crisis, it was thought that each department could do what was needed without delay. And if every department did their job, the City as a whole would recover faster. Never did anyone imagine we'd get to test this theory in a pandemic.

Now to get a permit, I needed the approval of the Commissioner of Public Safety, as he controlled the police and the fire departments. I also needed the approval of the Commissioner of Public Works because he controlled who used Congress Park where the fireworks were launched. I also needed the Commissioner of Accounts to approve the permit and to provide insurance. With money to pay for the services provided by each department as well as the fireworks, they all said yes.

So after I left my mom on her first day at the Wesley, I went to my office to prepare a statement to let the community know the fireworks were saved. Later that afternoon while I stood at the podium in front of television cameras to make this announcement, I could feel my cell phone vibrating inside my suit jacket. After I answered the last question, I looked at my phone and realized it was my mom. Because I knew how much she liked to play games on her phone, I had left it with her. That was a big mistake.

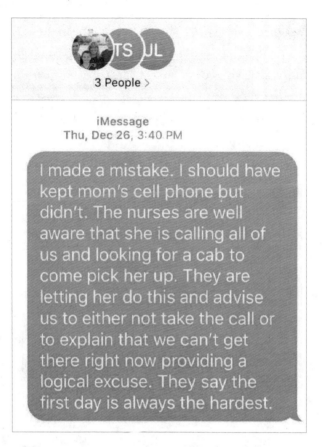

When my mom was diagnosed with Alzheimer's, the burden of her care fell first on my sister Tracy because my mom lived with her family. Tracy was with her the day the neurologist gave my mom this diagnosis, and every appointment after that. My mom was a nurse for 48 years, so she knew what this meant. Tracy later told me, "She was so scared. I also know she was scared for me."

Tracy cared for our mom when she fell and shattered her elbow. It was Tracy who took her car away when she started to get lost. Tracy organized her doctor visits, medication, daily schedule and finances. She made sure my mom was eating, sleeping and safely taking her daily walks with Ribbie.

During this time in my mom's Alzheimer's journey, I was the fun one. I swooped into town occasionally for Chamber business and to visit with her. Lisa and I drove down a few times when Tracy and her family went on vacation, and sometimes we arranged for her to visit with us. Early on, she could fly to Saratoga by herself. But on her last flight, my mom became disoriented as the plane took off. A flight attendant came to her rescue, assured her that she'd be okay and escorted her to find me when the plane landed.

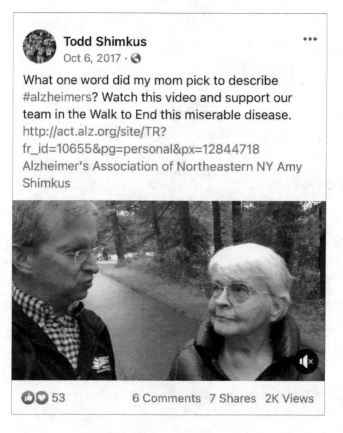

Two years ago, in 2017, I signed the two of us up to participate in the Walk to End Alzheimer's. To raise money, we did a video together. Before I shot the video, I told my mom that we would play a game where I would say a word and she had to say the first word that came into her mind. We practiced a few times, and I used silly words that made her laugh before she answered. I then told her I was going to turn the camera on and we'd play the game for real.

"Okay, here's the first word. Todd," I said. She replied, "Son."

"Here's the second word, Ribbie," I said. She replied. "Dog," with a big smile on her face. Ribbie is a small white bichon frise. From the first time Tracy brought him home, Ribbie spent all day every day with mom. To keep track of where she was at all times, Tracy attached a monitor to Ribbie's collar. She knew mom might forget her purse or her cell phone, but there was no chance she would leave the dog behind.

In the summer of 2019, my mom went to live with her older sister, Joanie, in Massachusetts. By this time, my mom needed someone to be with her 24/7. We didn't think she was ready for a nursing home just yet, and Joanie always said that my mom was welcome to live with her. None of us knew how long this might work.

When she moved to Joanie's, the real Ribbie stayed with Tracy. This separation would have been traumatic except for a little ingenuity from Trisha. She bought my mom a stuffed animal that looked just like Ribbie. To my amazement, this stuffed animal and my mom also became inseparable. She sat in her chair and watched television with him. When she went for a drive with Joanie and to bed at night, she carried this stuffed Ribbie with her. I would soon learn how common this is for individuals with dementia.

When we made our fundraising video before the 2017 Alzheimer's walk, I correctly predicted what she would say when I said Todd or Ribbie. But what I really wanted to know was how she'd answer the third word I planned to ask her.

"Okay, here's the next word, Alzheimer's," I said to my mom as the video rolled on. Without hesitation, my mom looked at me and replied, "Miserable." She then paused and added, "I'd like to use another word but I probably shouldn't say that on video." Then we both laughed, but as I would learn later no truer words were ever said. Now whenever I see, hear or write the word Alzheimer's, the word miserable is the first word I think of too.

In many ways, I believe Alzheimer's can be more miserable for those of us who love and care for those who have the disease. For someone with Alzheimer's, those moments that are miserable come and go. For instance, my mom soon forgot pleading with me not to leave her at Wesley, but I will never forget that moment. Nor will I forget what she did that day that caused my cell phone to go crazy.

Unable to escape, my mom called every contact in her cell phone. It was a basic human instinct: she couldn't flee so she had to fight. My mom wanted to go home and she asked everyone who answered the call to help her. After she spoke to them, they called or texted me and hoped I could do something. I walked outside of the Saratoga Arts Center and immediately called my mom's nurse.

"Hi Todd, we're well aware of the calls your mom is making," she told me calmly. "This is normal behavior. The first day can be tough. If she calls again, tell her you cannot get there right away but that you'll be there as soon as you can. By the way, your mom managed to call a cab company too," the nurse said.

I chuckled as I thought about how that conversation with the cab company must have gone. She didn't know where she was. If they monitored where the call was coming from, they'd think she called from Virginia. They would have been lost too.

Yet I was also in awe of her resilience. She did whatever she had to do so that Tracy, Trisha and I always had what we needed. Today, on December 26, 2019, she didn't have what she needed and couldn't reach us. So she called a cab to take her home.

As her Alzheimer's progressed, she often became anxious and wanted to know where the kids were. In her mind, she was always with them at some point that day. When she couldn't find them, she called us and asked: "Where are the kids? Are the kids with you?"

None of us ever figured out what kids she was looking for. Was she talking about her three children or her six grandchildren? Could it have been her siblings? When we asked, she often said she was look-

ing for the "kids who were just here." This happened at Tracy's house, Joanie's, and mine too. Sometimes she might use a name or two but it was never consistent.

In September of 2019, Joanie dropped my mom off at their sister's, Betty's house, to run an errand. A short time later, my mom asked Betty where the kids were. When Betty said there were no kids there, my mom got upset and pushed Betty out of the way so she could leave to look for them. "She was too strong," Betty told me. "I couldn't stop her."

In early December, my mom was with us in Saratoga. A major winter storm hit and snow fell at a rate of one to two inches per hour. Later in the afternoon, my mom was agitated and she whirled around our house looking for the kids. Normally, I was a calming influence, but not this time. She put on her coat, grabbed her pocket book and dog, and walked out my back door to look for her car so she could go find the kids.

I didn't fight her, instead I put on my coat and followed. She walked down the driveway and turned right and kept walking. She had no idea where she was or where she was going, but she was in no mood to listen to me. As I followed a safe distance behind, my mom trudged through this blizzard for nearly two blocks until she finally came to a stop. I called Lisa to come get us as I walked up to my mom.

I convinced her to get into the car only because she agreed with me that Ribbie might be cold. He was covered in snow as we all were. When we got back to our house, she stormed in and sat on the couch. That's when she called me on her phone, as I stood in the other room and let her leave me a voicemail.

"Hey Todd, I want to come back to the house," my mom said, her voice trembling either from the cold or the fear. "But I have somebody here holding me prisoner because he won't do anything with me. I'm at Todd's, please call me back."

I was simultaneously the one she called to save her and the person that held her hostage. This was a call to action for me. What if she did this at Joanie's house, at night out in the woods? Like Betty, there was no chance Joanie could have stopped her, nor could Joanie follow my mom into the woods that surrounded her house.

The next day I called the Wesley to start the application process. They advise me that there was a waiting list, and there was no promise as to when a room might open. But two weeks later a room was available and they wanted her to move in right away. I asked them if we could delay this until right after Christmas so she could see her extended family one more time. As her legal guardian, I signed all the paperwork and never said a word to her.

Most of the Shimkus, Duvfa and Wehkoja families gathered at Betty's house on December 24, 2019. This family tradition extended back more than five decades. This was where we always gathered on Christmas eve, to enjoy dinner, a visit from Santa, and a gift exchange.

Tracy and her family were not with us this year, as they scheduled a cruise for the Holiday. They would be my mom's first visitors after the New Year. For most family members gathered there, because of events no one could have predicted, this was when they said goodbye to my mom and the last time they saw her alive.

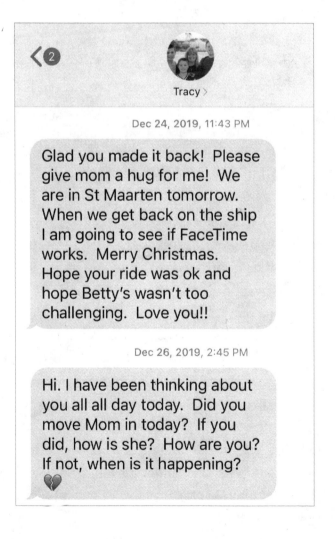

"It's just so sad," Joanie's daughter, my cousin Jen, said. "All the good folks get a crappy deal. I love your mom. This sucks." Later that night, Trisha said on Facebook: "Mom, I hope the memories you are able to retain are those of love and happiness. God, I don't know why you did this to my mom."

After the party was over, my mom and I drove to my home. She stayed awake the entire three hour drive, as we listened to Christmas music. Lisa and Katie were awake and helped my mom to get settled. By this time, my mom had already forgotten that she spent time earlier that Christmas Eve with her family.

On December 27 and her second day at the Wesley, instead of a call from my mom, I got a call from her social worker. "Your mom has made friends with one of the people in the cafeteria," she advised. "She talks a lot about being a nurse and Ribbie."

Two days later, on December 29, I was advised that it was okay for me to visit, and we were reunited. My plan was to visit her every day, never thinking for one second about whether or not a public health emergency might alter this plan. Like every person who loves someone with Alzheimer's, I was concerned that she'd forget who I was if she didn't see me regularly. I also believed she'd get better care if I got to know the staff and helped them as much as I could.

When our first visit ended, I escorted my mom to the cafeteria for lunch so she would not be alone. I again told her I had to go to work and gave her a hug. This time, she asked me when I would be back and I told her as soon as possible. As I left the cafeteria, I went to her room and grabbed her cell phone. If my mom really needed to talk to me or anyone else, the nurse assured me that she'd let her use a phone on the floor.

The next day on my visit, she and I sat together and I organized a virtual visit for her with Joanie using FaceTime. They were both excited to see each other and my mom started to talk right away. Never once did I think that I too might have to rely on a virtual visit to spend time with my mom.

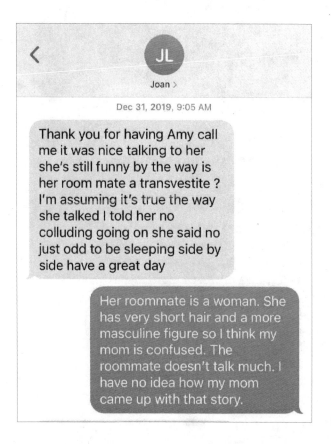

Each day, I watched as everyone on the staff called my mom, Nurse Amy. Like her stuffed animal dog, identifying her this way gave her life at the Wesley purpose. She still remembered being a nurse, and it was a job she loved. Now when I was not there, she was still able to take walks with her dog, and to do rounds on the floor as a nurse.

JANUARY 1, 2020

IT WAS 2020, A NEW YEAR. The start of a new decade. The night before, thousands visited the First Night locations where artists performed across Saratoga. Families came for the Fireworks too. Ryan and Darryl joined me in Congress Park to make sure they went off without a hitch. That night, I was hopeful and excited about 2020.

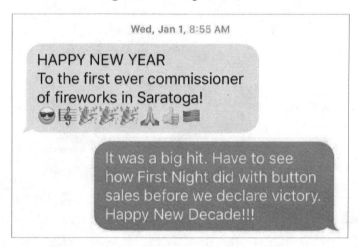

My mom was now a Saratogian, and a visit with her was added to my daily schedule. This was also a Leap Year, and this meant we all got an extra day, on February 29. Four years earlier, in 2016, our Chamber invented Leap of Kindness Day to give a new purpose to this extra day. Our idea was to encourage as many people as possible to spend their extra day doing something kind for someone else. In Saratoga, hundreds of people performed acts of kindness that helped thousands.

Now in 2020, I thought Leap of Kindness Day had tremendous potential to spread around the globe. We shared this idea with chambers everywhere and invited them to replicate our program in their communities. So for me, 2020 was destined to be a year of kindness - or so I thought.

What no one knew, on this first day of 2020, is that the World Health Organization (WHO) had some difficult questions for officials in Wuhan, China about a cluster of cases of pneumonia. No deaths were reported but this changed quickly. Without warning, a new virus was discovered and it began to spread. There was nothing kind about it.

Barbara Jordan and 13 others   4 Comments

On the second day of the new year, China said this was a "viral pneumonia of unknown cause." A week later, a preliminary determination announced this as a novel (or new) coronavirus. According to Chinese authorities, "the virus in question can cause severe illness in some patients and does not transmit readily between people."

I had no idea where Wuhan, China was. I did not pay any attention to this news. Today, I spent time with Tracy, Joel and Jared. They drove up from Virginia. Jared and Joel were on winter break. Jared was a senior at James Madison University studying to become a firefighter and Paramedic. Joel was a freshman at the same school studying hospitality management.

"Last week while we were on a cruise, a bed opened up in a memory care unit near my brother," Tracy wrote on Facebook. "It was so hard to not be there to help her. My brother moved her in the day after Christmas. Today was rough. But this morning we watched videos of our cruise and played with snap chat filters. My mom thought this was hilarious. We made it fun - and THIS I want to remember."

My mom recognized them. They each gave her a hug. There were no restrictions on visits so they stayed with her for hours. We had no clue how precious these in-person visits were. We figured my mom's Alzheimer's was the miserable disease that would traumatize her and us. Tracy and I hoped to spend more time together for as long as our mom lived here in Saratoga. The virus had other ideas.

When our mom went into the Wesley, I hoped to take her out to go places and do things together to create more memories to cherish. For instance, Trisha and I talked about mom and I traveling to one of Tyler's basketball games. He deserved this opportunity to spend time with his Mimi.

Until this was possible, Trisha suggested using our Facebook portals to allow my mom to watch Tyler's games virtually and she sent me the schedule. From that point forward, I scheduled my Saturday visits so we could watch the games. When they ended, Tyler came right up to the screen and said hi to his Mimi.

"You make me smile when I see your face on the Portal," Trisha wrote in a note she mailed to our mom. "You have made it to every game, and Tyler is always excited to speak with you. Tyler and I love you so much and we can't wait to see you soon."

This inspired me to schedule virtual visits every Sunday for my mom's sisters. Joanie did not feel up to traveling and Betty would not do so alone. Joanie had my mom's portal now and she knew how to use it. My mom clearly enjoyed the chance to see and talk to people she loved and recognized. It was a small break for me too, in that she had something to do other than just talking and walking with me.

But virtual visits had their limitations. In person, she'd give and get a hug from me. I always brought food to share, a cup of coffee, a chocolate chip cookie, or a blueberry muffin. She smiled and had an excited look on her face when I'd show her what I brought for her each day. If I said something sarcastic, she might give me a look that said, yeah right, and we'd laugh together. If her dog was missing, I looked for it and made sure she had it before I left.

Saying goodbye was easier in person. It just seemed awkward and sudden online. Sometimes she didn't hear Joanie, Trisha or Tyler say I love you at the end of the virtual visit, and she didn't reciprocate. In person, I could repeat this until she understood and told me she loved me too.

Trisha and Tyler visited our mom in person on January 20, and Betty and Trisha visited in person on February 20. We all believed regular and consistent contact with the people she loved was important to her health and quality of life. She was no longer living with anyone in her family. Her real dog was in Virginia. She suffered enough loss already. I didn't want her there alone, not for one day.

The day after Trisha and Tyler's visit was on what would have been my parent's 54th wedding anniversary. Had my mom not had Alzheimer's, she and I could have talked about that special day during my visit. Perhaps she could have shared how they met or how long they dated. Maybe she would have described how and where my dad asked her to marry him. She didn't remember any of this now.

I just knew that my mom, Amy Wehkoja, married my dad, Herb Shimkus, on January 21, 1966. My dad was a barber and owned his own shop. They had three children with blonde hair and blue eyes. We were like most American families, with one big exception: my mom worked the graveyard shift, from 11 p.m. to 7 a.m. I can't imagine how hard it must have been for my mom to work the night shift. This schedule worked to raise children, not as much for themselves as husband and wife.

All three of us kids did well in school and graduated from private colleges. We are all confident, independent, and work hard. I think that I get my practicality from my mom and my creativity from my dad. My mom, by example, showed us how to care for others. My dad took risks and had a lot of fun. Over time, these two paths diverged.

My mom and dad stayed together until my junior year in high school, in 1984. This was also not unusual in the 1980's. Approximately fifty percent of first-marriages ended in divorce then. It was entirely amicable, and they remained friends. My mom kept my dad on her health and life insurance plan. They traveled together to our school and extracurricular events and later did the same to be at birthday parties for their grandchildren.

My dad passed away, in 1999, from a heart attack caused by a lifetime smoking cigarettes. He started when he was sixteen and never stopped. He did not feel well for more than a year before his death. When he went to the doctor, my mom went with him. She went with everyone in the family to see the doctor. Nurse Amy knew what questions to ask and what to tell us to do.

The doctor told my dad he was in trouble, that he needed heart surgery. At Ben's fifth birthday party, my dad talked to Lisa's dad about this diagnosis. Lisa's dad, Richard Davis, survived heart surgery one year earlier. He had recuperated at our home. We were ready to make the same offer to my dad. Lisa's dad told him to get it done, but my dad never got the chance. A week later, on May 13, my dad died at just 55 years old.

My mom retired just before she was diagnosed with Alzheimer's. She did so to help Tracy to care for her children and because she was tired of working. Being a mom, a nurse, and now Grammy Amy were the three most important things in her life. I was the first of her three children born a little more than a year after she and my dad were married, on April 18, 1967.

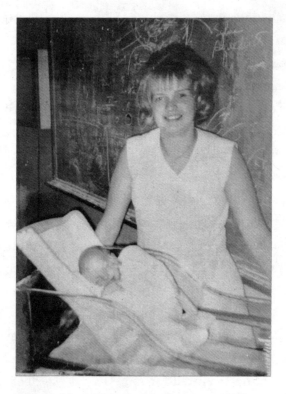

I was born at Holden Hospital, where my mom worked, with a life-threatening birth defect, called an omphalocele. An omphalocele is where internal organs are outside of the body. They can be small or large. Mine was huge, with all of my abdominal organs in a sack outside of my stomach.

"Within minutes, Todd was in an ambulance with a police escort headed to Boston," my dad told his friends about my birth. "It was a ninety minute drive. They had Todd at Mass General Hospital in forty-five minutes. Doctor Hardy Hendren was there and they told me they needed to do emergency surgery or else he'd die. I had no choice and signed the papers."

It took nine operations over my first ten months of life, and I spent nearly that entire time at the Hospital. "Four times, we were told that Todd was not likely to make it," my dad said when he told this story. "Doctor Hendren saved him. It was a miracle."

I never again required surgery, and thankfully there have been no complications since. But beyond the heroics performed by the medical professionals, there was another part of my dad's story I never forgot. "When Todd was in the hospital, Amy and I went to visit him nearly every day. When we left the hospital, we bought bleacher seats to see the Red Sox and we saw almost all of their home games."

It was a ninety minute drive. This didn't stop them from visiting me while my dad ran the Holden Barber Shop and my mom was a nurse. When I needed them, they were there. Now I was paying it forward as I visited my mom every day. I only had to drive a mile to get there.

I played baseball through little league and basketball until high school. My dad taught me to body surf in the ocean. My grandfather, and my mom's dad, Benny, taught me to golf. I played on the high school team. I loved sports and even played tackle football when my friends decided that was the game of choice in our neighborhood.

In 1979, when I was 12 years old, my mom and I went for my annual checkup with Dr. Hendren. I told him I played baseball and basketball. He advised that this was too dangerous, that just one hit to my stomach could do real damage. I didn't have the protection other kids had. After this visit, he sent a letter directly to my school and told them it was not safe for me to play any contact sport.

Growing up, there were times when I was hit in the stomach by a ball or an elbow. No doubt it took my breath away and scared me every time, but I was not ready to give up sports. Cautious parents would have followed Dr Hendren's orders, but my parents didn't right away. Instead they taught me resilience as we got a second opinion and looked for options.

Our local physician consulted with an orthopedic doctor. Within a couple of days, they wrapped my abdominal area in a cast to take a mold of my stomach. Using this mold, they built a hard plastic protective shell that looked like a helmet that fit tightly over my stomach. They then secured a small adjustable back brace that I could use to keep the protective brace in place during games. I called it my belly hat, and it allowed me to play basketball in middle school and sports with my friends, even as an adult.

I was so mad at Dr. Hendren that I never went to see him again. My parents said this was my decision to make. But as I got older, I often thought about this with some regret. Not that I felt like I needed his medical advice, but instead I really felt that it was unkind of me to never return to thank him for saving my life.

Thirty seven years after my last visit with Dr. Hendren, I found myself on stage at our Chamber's annual dinner, in January of 2016. In my speech to our 900 guests, I introduced for the first time our plan to host Leap of Kindness Day, on February 29, 2016.

To make it easy for everyone to participate, we put a blank Leap of Kindness Day card at all of the place settings. I held one up at the podium and told everyone to take the card we gave them to write a thank you note to someone who had made a difference in their life. Once I said this out loud, I silently said to myself: practice what you preach and send a thank you note to Dr Hendren.

The next day, I went online and learned that he had created the Hendren Foundation. I reached out to the executive director who was kind enough to call me a few days later. Dr. Hendren was 90 years old, alive and well, and always interested to hear from former patients. She gave me his address so I could send him a thank you note. She also shared his phone number with me so I could call and talk with him on February 29, 2016.

"Hi Todd, I remember you," Dr. Hendren said to me when I called him. "I got your card. You should come see me. I have your file in my basement."

In addition to my medical file, Dr. Hendren also had the thank you card that I mailed to him one week earlier. Inside, I wrote him a short note, and I hoped he remembered me. Now I knew he did and I thanked him for saving my life and I promised to visit him.

In 2017, I kept my promise and decided to bring my mom with me. We drove three hours together to get to his home on the Atlantic coast. Just minutes before we arrived, I told my mom who we were going to see. "Really, I haven't seen him in a long time," she said. "How did you find him? How old is he now?"

When Doctor Hendren came to the door, he wore glasses almost exactly like mine. He was dressed in khaki pants just like me, and a yellow sweater over a blue and white checkered button down shirt.

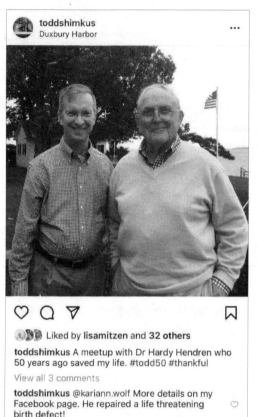

So even his shirt was almost identical to what I wore. I took it as a sign of our special connection.

"You're not the first person Hardy saved that has visited," his wife said. "He has performed life saving surgeries on every continent except Antarctica. Next week, there are doctors coming from Japan to get his advice."

In his basement, he kept files from all of his patients. He had gone to great lengths to take lots of photos and to keep great notes. He captured these moments to teach others what he learned about each procedure. He was one of the best pediatric physicians in the world. I was lucky our paths crossed, in 1967, and again fifty years later.

The four of us sat down at their dining room table. Dr. Hendren handed me a file with my name on it. There were papers with scribbled notes and other typed papers that looked more official. I shuffled through them and stopped when I came to the pictures.

I looked at the first one carefully. I couldn't stop looking at it except to show it to my mom. She looked but didn't say a word. This was the first time I saw what I looked like on the day I was born. It was not anything like most first day baby photos. In mine, I'm all alone, naked, lying on my back on a table. I look like a normal baby with two arms and two legs, my hands drawn toward my face. I have two eyes, two ears, one nose and one mouth. I was cute.

Except that I had what looked like an umbilical cord that extended out from my stomach. This cord went from my body to an oval shaped mass. Inside of this mass sitting right outside of this baby's body, my body, were all of my internal abdominal organs. They were in this sack entirely outside my body.

There were three more photos in the file that showed the progress Dr. Hendren made as he treated me. The next must have been soon thereafter as this mass was now partially inside my body. In the next photo, the mass was even further inside of me. Then in the fourth and final photo, I was again on my back with my stomach completely sewn up. I could see the stitches. The mass of internal organs once outside my body were now inside. Looking at these photos, I finally saw what Dr. Hendren did to save me. It really was a miracle.

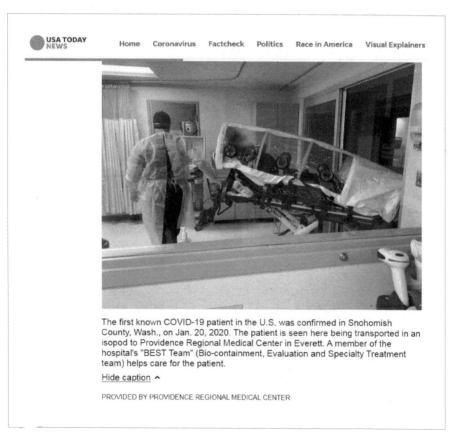

The first known COVID-19 patient in the U.S. was confirmed in Snohomish County, Wash., on Jan. 20, 2020. The patient is seen here being transported in an isopod to Providence Regional Medical Center in Everett. A member of the hospital's "BEST Team" (Bio-containment, Evaluation and Specialty Treatment team) helps care for the patient.

Hide caption ˄

PROVIDED BY PROVIDENCE REGIONAL MEDICAL CENTER

My mom said little during the visit. She clearly remembered that Doctor Hendren was the person who saved my life. She hugged him before we left and said thank you. She didn't mention him again on the drive back to Saratoga or ever again as far as I know.

On January 21, 2020, a US resident tested positive for the virus after he returned from Wuhan, China, and doctors everywhere would soon begin to search for a miracle to save the lives of their patients. When asked if he was concerned, President Trump responded: "No, not at all. And we have it totally under control. It's one person coming in from China. It's going to be just fine."

The Center for Disease Control (CDC) also said the risk was low. They admitted the illness resulted in several deaths, but advised that "other patients have had milder illness and been discharged." The only concern they mentioned was that it appeared the virus spread from person to person.

Two days later, the Chamber hosted our 102nd Annual Dinner. Not one of the 800 attendees considered wearing a mask. Two weeks later, Discover Saratoga hosted its 36th annual Chowderfest. Thirty thousand people consumed 120,000 cups of chowder. This mass of humanity stood in line outside of participating restaurants to get their $1 samples. No one thought to stand six feet apart. A week later, the City Center welcomed 10,000 people for the annual Dance Flurry. No one was asked to use hand sanitizer, to take a rapid test, or to have their temperature taken before they entered the facility.

No special precautions were taken by St. Mary's School either when they hosted their annual volleyball game between the teachers and students. Everyone gathered after the game as the principal announced that Lisa was selected by her peers as the Teacher of the Year.

My mom was a great nurse, and my wife, Lisa, was a great teacher. Working in a Catholic School for 15 years now, she spent most of her salary on supplies and often said: "I work to support my teaching habit."

Lisa is meticulous about her classroom. Everything has to match, and there is always a theme with educational decorations everywhere. During the past summer, she and another teacher created a new science and technology lab. They also reconfigured the school's library.

Lisa taught fifth grade and absolutely deserved this honor. The plan was to honor her at the school's Parent Prom in June. "I love working with kids," Lisa said. "I'm just not comfortable being the center of attention in front of so many people." This anxiety would soon be the least of her worries.

"When I need to talk to someone, I call mom. When I need an answer, I call dad," is one of my favorite Katie quotes. I'm not good with drama. I always jump to taking action. That can be helpful when Katie or Ben have questions about finances, apartments, careers or dealing

with the media. Thankfully Lisa is a good listener, so she's the one Katie and Ben call when they just want to talk, vent or cry.

Lisa and I are proud of the fact that Katie and Ben have always been close. Ben always adored his older sister, and Katie has always been incredibly protective of her "little" brother. Both are smart, creative and care about other people. Katie loves reading, photography, yoga, cycling and writing. Ben loves music, cars, tumbling and football. Katie is my buddy when it comes to coffee and beer. Ben is the one I call to talk about the New England Patriots or what car I should buy.

Lisa and I love to travel with them. When they were young, we'd take them on what they called "social studies" vacations to Washington D.C., Boston, New York City, and Philadelphia. The four of us went to Ireland in 2004. For my fiftieth birthday, in 2017, we went to Chicago to see the musical Hamilton and a Cubs game at Wrigley Field.

By late January 2020, the four of us had not been together since November 9, 2019. On that day, Lisa and I drove to Boston. Katie lived nearby in Somerville, and she had just started a new job as a Bookseller with the MIT Press. Ben was a performer on a cruise ship that made a stop in Boston.

As soon as we learned that Ben had permission to leave the ship, we made plans to get all of us together. Lisa and I booked a hotel. Katie and Ben met us there. We had dinner at a Vegan restaurant Katie picked just for Ben.

"It was great to see you guys," Ben texted me. "Mom is still crying," I texted back. Once Ben returned to the cruise ship, we would not see him again until March. As he cruised around the Bahamas, he called whenever he could find WiFi. But we missed being with him, especially during the holidays.

Ben's contract ended March 11, and I booked him a flight from Miami to Saratoga on that day. Lisa and I wanted to be reunited with him as soon as possible. We asked Katie to book a train so she could join us that weekend.

Lisa and I made our own travel plans to visit London during April's school vacation. Katie and Ben volunteered to watch our dog, Sammi. They would take my place and visit Grammy Amy while we were gone.

The virus traveled too, as it spread from one person to another and from one country to another. In February, crew members and guests on cruise ships were among the first to get and die from the virus. In the US, the virus surged first in nursing homes. My mom and Ben were both in harm's way. Eventually, we all were.

FEBRUARY 2020

The Chamber was off to a great start in this new year, so was Saratoga's economy. The Chamber opened a second office, and I hired two new employees. These were sound decisions at the time, but I would soon question whether we could afford these new expenses.

We held ribbon cuttings to celebrate the opening of a new brewery and coffee shop, a new pizza joint, and the new headquarters for a local cleaning company. For the brewery and pizza joint, this dream soon became a nightmare. For the cleaning company, they'd soon realize a surge in business. The virus threatened the very existence of some businesses, while it proved to be profitable for others.

For now, the virus didn't factor into any decisions we made. "Even though there are no confirmed cases of novel coronavirus in New York, we continue to take every precaution necessary," Governor Cuomo said. New York's Health Commissioner added, "It is important for people to take appropriate precautions, just as they should to protect themselves against the flu, and have confidence that we are prepared."

Some of the first people to realize we were not prepared were the crew and passengers on cruise ships, like the Diamond Princess. In February, one passenger from China left this ship and tested positive for the virus. This one case led to an outbreak that infected more than 700 people, and 14 passengers died.

The World Dream cruise ship with more than 3,000 people was quarantined off the coast of China. The Grand Princess was stopped on the coast of California. More than 100 people on this ship tested positive, and 7 passengers perished. As we saw these news reports, Lisa and I became increasingly concerned for Ben. He assured us that no one on his ship was sick, but this didn't make us feel any better.

Katie was not in harm's way, from the virus at least. On the surface, it appeared things were going well. Her first novel was on-sale online and in our local bookstore. The store featured it on a display of books written by local authors. "I wonder if I can get the author to sign this book for me," I said in a post after I purchased her book.

As an employee at MIT, Katie received a free MBTA pass to travel the city. She had her bike, camera, and laptop and often found time to explore, take photos, read and write. Her partner lived in Boston too, so they spent time together. But her apartment was expensive and she didn't get along with her roommates. She had always been challenged with time management and felt stressed by an increasing number of responsibilities. Turning 30 this year, Katie thought a lot about her future, so Lisa decided to visit with her to see if we could help.

When Lisa returned, she said I needed to help Katie find a new place to live. A week later, Katie found an apartment she liked that was more affordable and closer to the bookstore. She listed her apartment and immediately scheduled two showings. "This will work out," I texted her. "It is just a few moving parts that ideally will all fit together. And if not, it is only money and we have that. No stress. Seriously."

She got out of the old apartment lease and signed a new one that was less expensive. Lisa and I promised to help her move, on Sunday, March 1 - one day after Leap of Kindness Day. Thanks to the virus, Katie spent just two weeks in this new apartment.

The lines between what I do for work and what I do in my personal life often blurred. In 2011, Katie sent me a link to a continuous music video, called a Lip Dub, produced by the students at Emerson, where she got her bachelor's degree. I showed it to the Chamber's communications person and suggested we do a Saratoga Lip Dub. In late August of 2012, more than 1,500 people, horses, and dogs appeared in this local video.

Now, in 2020, as we approached Leap of Kindness Day, I noticed that my mom was not the only resident that carried a stuffed animal. Even those who didn't carry one often had a stuffed dog, cat, bear, pig or rabbit on their bed or dresser. They'd all pet my mom's dog when she let them. She sometimes now had one of their animals on her bed too.

This inspired me to ask the Chamber's staff if they'd help me organize a stuffed animal drive for Leap of Kindness Day. The goal was to deliver as many stuffed animals to the Wesley for them to distribute to residents as possible. Once everyone agreed, I took a photo of my mom with her dog, making her and Ribbie the public face of this act of kindness in Saratoga.

"I'm going to make you famous," I told her after I took this photo. "We will share this picture of you and Ribbie with the world." My mom laughed when I said this. She rolled her eyes when I told her Ribbie would be famous too. "Oh really," she said with a hint of sarcasm.

I posted this photo of them on social media, and it was shared by the Wesley, the Chamber, our staff and my sisters. A collection box was set up in the Chamber's lobby. Two local stores put out collection boxes to support our effort. Friends began to drop off or ship stuffed animals to us. The need for these companions would soon be greater than ever before.

When my mom wasn't posing for promotional photos, she spent a considerable amount of time walking the halls of 2 Victoria. This was Nurse Amy in action. She was doing rounds, checking on her patients. There were times on our walks when she'd go into another resident's room to check up on them. "Are you okay," she'd ask. They'd either stay silent or mumble something back to her. "I will be right back."

In February, the staff gave her a stethoscope, and she was invited to sit in the nurses station. The staff was urged to acknowledge her expertise and to ask her for advice on things like how to change a bed. She'd sit at the nurses desk, next to the living room and watch what people said and did. She'd write down what she observed and give her report to the nurse when asked. It didn't matter that what she wrote made no sense. They called this a "therapeutic fib" but it made her feel valued and this kept her busy.

"Hey Amy, here's your son again," her friend Judy said whenever I arrived. Judy seemed more alert than most. She was the only resident who greeted me every day. Judy had dark black hair and a raspy voice, and wore t-shirts with Elvis's face on them. She told me she met Elvis once. When I wore a suit and tie to visit, Judy said, "Your son must have something important to do today."

My mom's other close friend was Antoinette. She was quiet, rail thin, with really short brown hair. When she did talk, she always shared the same story about a time when she was kicked by a horse. "Were you hurt?" I asked her. "No. Not really," she'd reply. Then she'd giggle a little. It was impossible to determine if this was true. Antoinette was the first person my mom let hold her dog, a sure sign my mom trusted her.

My mom told me stories about what she did to help the "patients." She'd complain about how some of the other "nurses" handled a particular situation, and often confused the other residents as lazy because they didn't work as much as she did. "Your mom's very alert," the real nurse told me. "She's watching us all the time. When we have a problem with a resident, I look at your mom and she'll roll her eyes. It's very cute."

Nurses everywhere were soon on the front line in our war with this virus. By mid-February, there were 40,000 confirmed cases in the world. Because of a shortage of tests, there were likely tens of thousands more who had the virus but didn't know.

Nearly all of these cases were in China. The WHO said this virus was called COVID-19. Under WHO guidelines, they "had to find a name that did not refer to a geographical location, an animal, an individual or a group of people." That didn't stop President Trump from repeatedly calling it the "China-virus."

On March 1, 2020, New York State confirmed its first case of COVID-19 among our 19-million residents. One day later, the New York Times quoted Governor Cuomo: "We think we have the best health care system on the planet here in New York. So, when you're saying, what happened in other countries versus what happened here, we don't even think it's going to be as bad as it was in other countries."

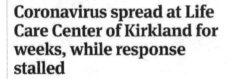

4 of 7 | Freshly suited up, a SERVPRO cleaning team re-enters... (Ken Lambert / The Seattle Times) More

By Asia Fields and Mary Hudetz

Seattle Times staff reporters

On February 28, a resident of a long term care facility in Washington State tested positive. Within two weeks, more than 120 residents, staff and visitors at this facility had the virus. Nearly forty died. I watched video of family members outside of these homes as they waved through windows to their relatives inside as they waved back.

These families were separated, unable to talk, hug or be together. Crews in hazardous material suits were sent in to clean and disinfect these facilities. They had no way to know who had the virus or how to stop its spread.

With my mom in a nursing home, I was concerned, but naively confident that this could never happen at the Wesley. I trusted the leaders and staff there, and knew they were likely taking whatever precautions were required. It never dawned on me that I too might one day have to visit my mom through a window.

The virus spread from person to person anywhere large numbers of people lived or gathered, like nursing homes, cruise ships, schools, offices and densely populated cities. We didn't know any of this in late-February or even early March. There really was no warning.

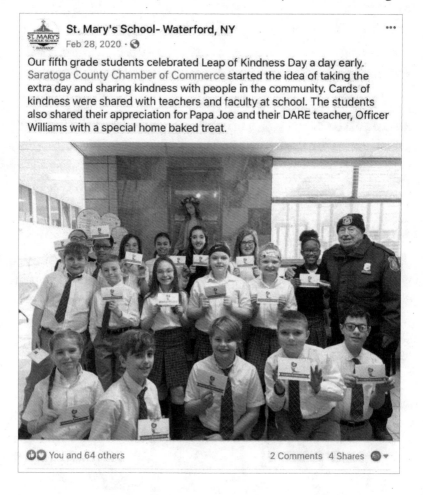

Lisa was prepared for Leap of Kindness Day. I gave her a supply of our blank Leap of Kindness Day cards, and she turned them into a writing assignment. Each student wrote something kind to someone who worked at the school, from another teacher to the 90-year old crossing guard, Papa Joe.

The school took a photo of Lisa's students holding their cards before they were delivered. Dressed in their school uniforms, the students had smiles, not masks, on their faces. They stood side by side inside a classroom where the windows were closed, not opened to allow fresh air to circulate.

Soon, no one was happy. Not the school principal, teachers, parents and certainly not the students. No one was ready for how quickly and completely this school year changed. There were 80 days of school left, but Lisa and her fifth-grade students would be together in person for just 10 of them.

On Leap of Kindness Day, I got a text early in the morning from my cousin Jen, that said: "Good morning. So you create this fantastic leap of kindness day that has spread all over and I learn that my state is one of only three not participating. What the hell is up with that. I can't believe you haven't been on a morning show yet with how much it has spread." What she didn't know was that I was on every morning show here in Saratoga.

I did three live interviews at local television stations the morning of February 29. As I entered the third studio, the set included two chairs where the anchor and I sat, a small glass table and a near life-size photo as the backdrop. I stopped in my tracks when I saw the photo.

It was the one we took with my mom, the Chamber staff and the Wesley's leaders and many of the stuffed animals people donated to us. I asked the camera person to take a picture of the reporter and me as we sat on the set in front of this photo.

In the photo, my mom and I sat together on a bench right in the center. She held Ribbie and a large pink rabbit. "Ok that makes me

cry. Couldn't love this any more," Tracy replied after she saw this photo. Here was proof that my mom and I could still enjoy moments together that were worth remembering, and this made me feel better about the decision to place her in the Wesley.

Chambers in 47 states participated in this year's Leap of Kindness Day, as did a dozen more across Canada, and one in Ireland. People collected food, clothes, toys, and personal care items. Leap of Kindness Day helped seniors, children, single mothers, soldiers, veterans, victims of sexual abuse and those who were homeless. Everyone that participated or benefitted from these acts of kindness had the Saratoga County Chamber to thank.

Searching on social media for the hashtag #leapofkindnessday, I scrolled through hundreds of posts and marveled at the impact. Some of the Chamber's staff and friends joined me at a brewery for dinner. With every beer we purchased, one dollar was donated to a local homeless shelter. We talked about how much bigger Leap of Kindness Day could be in 2024, and never once about the virus.

MARCH 1, 2020

IN MARCH, THE CDC ISSUED a recommendation: "Avoid all cruise travel due to the spread of COVID-19." No one told us to avoid big cities or anything else. So Lisa and I didn't think twice about driving to Boston to help Katie move.

That week, Massachusetts Governor Charlie Baker left with his family for a vacation. Like Governor Cuomo, he was unfazed by COVID-19. Before he left, Governor Baker said: "Massachusetts is home to world renowned hospitals and leading health care experts. The general public in Massachusetts remains at low risk."

What no one knew is that Boston was already under attack. In late-February, 175 people from all over the world gathered there for a conference. By March 1st, several were sick, and two days later, fifty attendees were symptomatic. This would be one of the first super-spreader events in the US.

From my experience with Dr. Hendren, I knew first hand how amazing the Massachusetts medical community could be. Like their peers in New York and across the world, they would soon be surprised and outmatched by the virus. The spread of the virus would be traumatic and the disruption it caused unprecedented.

During his senior year in college, in the Fall of 2015, Ben faced a traumatic situation, one that disrupted his life greatly and challenged his resilience. That's when a fellow student in the musical theater department at Cortland State University catfished him.

This student, Joey Gugliemeli, did this by creating a fake online persona, Allison Mossey. A mutual friend connected Ben and Allison, and Ben believed Allison was a producer at Playwrights Horizons in New York City. Ben was so excited; he called Lisa and I after he first spoke to

Allison. He wanted to know if it was okay for him to leave school if he got this part, and we answered yes. Allison and Ben exchanged more than 150 emails. As requested, Ben sent Allison audition videos, some that Ben later said felt particularly sexual and awkward.

Eventually, Ben contacted Playwrights Horizons and confirmed his suspicions. Allison wasn't real, and there was no show. It was a hoax, one that caused Ben such pain and confirmed Lisa's and my biggest fears for our son. Even when he was young, Lisa and I worried that he was too trusting, and that people would take advantage of him.

"You have to use your voice. You have to speak up for yourself," we told him often.

Now on March 4, 2020, Ben used his voice and took action against his abuser. In a Facebook post, he shared his catfishing story and how he experienced massive emotional trauma. "I consider the following months the lowest time for my mental health," Ben wrote.

He came out with his story solely to protect others from Joey, who was a contestant in RuPaul's Drag Race on VH1. Joey's stage name in this popular reality show was Sherry Pie, and the first episode was set to air on Friday, March 6. Ben warned everyone, "Sherry's success will bring her more opportunities to victimize other people."

Ben tagged no one in this post, nor did he ask anyone to share it. But thousands did, and I watched all day as the number of actions and comments reached into the thousands. Lisa and I both tried to reach Ben but he was out to sea. I knew how cruel social media could be so I set up Google alerts for Ben Shimkus, Sherry Pie, and RuPaul's Drag Race to track what was said.

Late on March 5, I got an alert and immediately read a story published on BuzzFeed that featured a photo of Ben and a link to his Facebook post. The reporter interviewed Ben and reviewed the emails from Allison that Ben kept. There were other victims who commented on Ben's post, and this reporter spoke to at least four other people who worked with Joey at other theaters who could prove Joey, Allison, or Sherry Pie catfished and traumatized them.

In 2015, when Ben brought this proof to college officials, they did nothing, as Joey had already left school. This BuzzFeed story triggered other media outlets to interview Ben and even more victims came forward. Now I wondered how Joey, RuPaul, and VH-1 would respond? We didn't have to wait long.

During the first 11 seasons of RuPaul's Drag Race, the show won 19 Emmys. Starting this week, Governor Cuomo held a daily COVID-19 update. Like Drag Race, these briefings became popular, nearly must-see television, especially if you lived in New York. He and a small team of his closest advisers understood how important it was as this crisis unfolded to share information with the public.

Later in 2020, these briefings received an Emmy. The Academy's president said: "The Governor's daily briefings worked so well because he effectively created television shows, with characters, plot lines, and stories of success and failure. People around the world tuned in to find out what was going on."

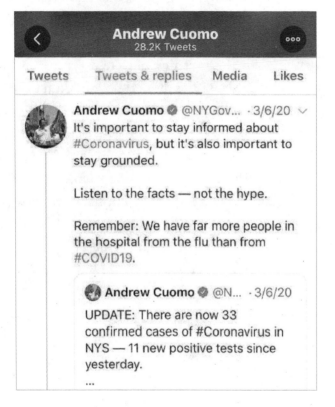

By March 6, there were nearly 100,000 confirmed cases of the virus in the world. There were thousands of people who were sick in South Korea, Italy and Iran. There were still only 150 confirmed cases in the US and just 30 in New York. This drastic under-counting - - most likely caused by a significant lack of tests - - enabled President Trump and Governor Cuomo to believe and talk as if there was nothing to fear.

"Listen to the facts. Not the hype," Governor Cuomo said on this day. "We have far more people in the hospital from the flu than from COVID 19."

On March 6, no one at the Wesley took my temperature or asked if I felt ill. No one asked if I had contact with anyone in the last ten days that had tested positive for COVID 19. I was never questioned whether I traveled out of state, and I was not required to wear a mask. As far as I could see, the only thing that looked different was Ribbie.

"What was Ribbie eating," I asked my mom. The fur around his mouth discolored, so it looked like he buried his nose in a bowl of pasta. "He went outside this morning. He likes to go out and play with the kids," she told me. She either didn't know or didn't remember if someone tried to feed him.

From there, I moved on to a meeting with Saratoga's Mayor and Ryan McMahon. The Mayor wanted us to help with First Night 2020, and we both said yes. He and I then attended a meeting with Saratoga's Public Safety Commissioner, Robin Dalton, where we were joined by Darryl, Deann, as well as Shelby Schneider, the head of Saratoga County Prosperity Partnership; and Samantha Bosshart of the Preservation Foundation. The six of us would soon begin to call ourselves the Saratoga Crew.

Commissioner Dalton was the daughter-in-law of Joe Dalton, my predecessor. On issues important to the Chamber, we expected her to collaborate with the business community. Today, we asked her to support a new law to tax guests that used online room rental platforms, like AirBnB and VRBO. We still thought this was our most pressing challenge, and as expected, she agreed to support our request.

After this meeting, I returned home where Lisa and I watched RuPaul's Drag Race for the first time to see what VH1 and RuPaul would say or do. That morning, Joey confessed: "I want to say how sorry I am that I caused such trauma and pain. I know what I did was wrong and truly cruel."

At 8 p.m., VH1 responded to the Sherry Pie admission of guilt and put up a fifty-two word statement. The white letters on the black screen stayed there just long enough for Lisa and me to read this statement. The station said that Sherry Pie was disqualified and she was banned from the grand finale to be filmed later.

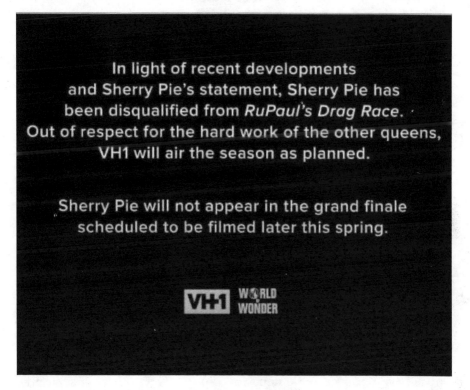

"Holy shit," I said to Lisa. I repeated this several times. "I can't believe it. They kicked Sherry Pie to the curb." Lisa was more interested to know what Ben thought. Was he satisfied? Did this action meet his expectations? He was still on the ship, so we didn't even know if he saw this.

Katie posted my favorite quote: "You know that scene in Love, Actually when Emma Thompson says her little brother just stood up for his country while she sewed a lobster costume? I'm sure I was up to something similarly ridiculous while Ben Shimkus was sharing his story and standing up for victims. Ben, only you could best a Queen, you fabulous fabulous thing."

But there was no apology from VH1 to the victims, and Sherry Pie actually won that first night's competition. The show's producers never admitted any guilt for failing to do a proper background check, nor did they take any action to help the victims.

RuPaul said absolutely nothing, not one word. Ben showed resilience as he told his story and set his trauma aside to help others, but RuPaul was a coward. Now every week, VH1 started each show with this black screen and vaguely worded message, while Sherry Pie performed and gained new fans.

Because of this, Ben was revictimized over and over again, and forced to defend himself from viewers who did not know the full story. One month later, Ben posted: "Last night, I received an Instagram DM wishing that someone would kill me. It is the fourth time this has happened. The hate I have received hasn't motivated me to stop talking, but it may silence others."

We were all about to experience trauma. Silently, COVID-19 spread more than anyone knew. Locally, the virus attacked first on March 7. That's when two Saratoga residents tested positive. New York City would soon be the epicenter of the virus' US arrival. My pandemic story started on Thursday, March 12. That was the day Lisa and I were reunited with Ben, and our entire family was separated from my mom. It all happened so fast.

THE WEEK OF MARCH 9TH

MONDAY MORNING, MARCH 9, my day started with a visit to a local Urgent Care facility. I was not sick or hurt, instead I was there for a scheduled meeting with hospital officials to talk about the need to expand public transportation services. We all shook hands, sat across a small table from one another, and none of us wore a mask.

"No one seemed concerned," I told everyone at the Chamber later that morning. "They told us that the region's hospitals are meeting daily to track local cases. If they were alarmed, our meeting would have been canceled."

Two days later, on March 11, 2020, the WHO declared COVID-19 a pandemic, and it quickly became far more pervasive, disruptive and deadly than the flu. This was a day full of ominous warnings, one where there was rampant speculation but few facts.

Visiting hours at the Wesley were reduced, and Tracy told me Jared and Joel were sent home from college for three weeks. The NBA suspended their season until further notice. A local union canceled their convention at the City Center. But late that night, there was one moment of pure joy for Lisa and me.

"Just landed," Ben texted me after midnight. Lisa and I were already at the airport. There was excitement and relief as we were reunited. He was off the ship, safe and healthy. But just moments before I hugged Ben, Brian Nealon, the Wesley's CEO called me and the news he shared was unbelievable.

"Hi Todd, I feel terrible calling you so late," Brian said. "Your mom is fine. We're now being told we need to suspend all non-essential visits. We don't know for how long. We will announce this tomorrow so you can still go see your mom in the morning."

I shared the news with Lisa. "Oh no," she said. "For how long? What are you going to do?" My mind was racing. What do I tell my sisters? What should I say to my mom? What could I do to make this easier for her? How long might this last? How bad is this virus?

I then watched as hundreds of people came through the security gate. When they saw their friends, family or loved ones, a smile appeared on their faces as they walked toward each other. There were hugs, kisses, and some tears of joy. No one hesitated to think that these simple gestures and close personal contacts might be spreading the virus. Neither did we.

When we saw Ben, Lisa and I smiled and waved enthusiastically to him. Lisa hugged him first and didn't want to let go. "Welcome back," I said. "Anything going on in your world?" I added. He just laughed. On the drive home, Lisa and Ben talked, but I didn't hear a word they said. I thought about my mom and how to leave her once again.

Lots of people would soon be told to stay away from loved ones. "There are now more than 118,000 cases in 114 countries, and 4,291 people have lost their lives," said WHO Director-General Dr. Tedros Adhanom Ghebreyesus. "Thousands more are fighting for their lives in hospitals. We are deeply concerned both by the alarming levels of spread and severity. We have never before seen a pandemic sparked by a coronavirus."

According to Governor Cuomo, more than 400 New York State residents tested positive for COVID 19 on March 12. We soon learned that asymptomatic people - those who experienced no ill effects from the virus - could be carriers. Not everyone that carried COVID-19 felt sick or had symptoms, which meant everyone we met or spent time with was a potential threat.

Governor Cuomo declared a State of Emergency, and announced that in-person gatherings were now limited to 500 people. "Why 500?," I thought to myself. To me, this seemed random. If we were seriously trying to stop the virus, shouldn't this number be a lot less?

For facilities with an occupancy of fewer than 500, the legal capacity was to be reduced by fifty percent. Local restaurants called to ask if this was fifty percent of room occupancy or fifty percent of seats. Hair salon owners and barbers called with the same question. Fitness facilities asked if this was fifty percent of room occupancy or fifty percent of the machines or class participants. Local stores wondered if they had to count the number of customers in their stores? Once again, I thought to myself, why fifty percent?

As the questions multiplied, I reached out to county leaders and local legislators. No one had any more details to share, and each advised that I watch the Governor's next briefing. The President of Saratoga Hospital offered me the best insight, "I will not be surprised if there is a business closure that comes out."

On Thursday morning, March 12th, I visited my mom before going to the chamber office. When I arrived, I brought her some gifts. They were going-away gifts. I was going away. Not by choice; that's for sure. This was the 75th day in a row I visited my mom. I really thought we'd be reunited in three weeks, maybe a month. No one could have imagined how long we'd be separated.

She got right up to give me a hug, and I presented the gifts to her one at a time: a cup of coffee, a chocolate chip cookie, an Amy for America sticker, and a new stuffed dog. She put the new dog on her lap immediately as they were instant friends.

"Hey Nurse Amy, did you get a new dog," a staff member asked. "What's his name? He looks smaller than Ribbie. Maybe you can call him Short Rib." The staff member and I laughed. My mom joined us, more to go along than because she understood the joke.

Giving her "Short Rib" was important. When I left her, Ribbie and Short Rib became my mom's best friends and her most loyal companions. These stuffed animals would be her only physical connection to her life outside of the Wesley. Instead of me, she'd take a walk with them each day. She'd visit and talk with them, not me.

Alzheimer's had stolen so much from my mom. COVID-19 and the forced and prolonged isolation of seniors in New York's nursing homes took so much more. This was the cruelest part of this virus: this was a time when my mom needed family contact the most and we couldn't be with her.

I didn't want to scare her, so I made the decision not to talk about the pandemic, or that my visits were about to stop. I had to appear to be myself, happy and hopeful. To be resilient in the face of this threat, I needed to focus on what I could do, not what was out of my control. The best I could do was to give her a new dog, a cup of coffee and a chocolate chip cookie. She loved all three, and I did it all with a smile.

When it was time for me to leave, she walked with me to the elevator. I wanted to take her with me. Leaving her today was so much harder than on her first day. "Todd, I'm not ready for this," she said then. Today, I wanted to say, "Mom, I'm not ready for this." Now it was me pleading silently to myself for her to come home with me.

But I knew she was in the safest place possible. My job would take me out into the community as soon as I left and every day thereafter. This is where the virus spread, and I couldn't go into lockdown with her. So I smiled like I did every day and gave her a hug. The hug might have been just a little longer than usual. If it was, she didn't notice.

"I have to go to work but I will see you soon," I said. That is what I was trained to say at the end of every visit. This way, she'd know that I would return. Then, I got into the elevator. It always took a little time for the doors to close. I think they programmed this delay in case a resident tried to leave.

I looked out at my mom, and she watched me as I just stood there. The doors didn't move, so I put my hands up to my face with my thumbs against my cheeks and my fingers outstretched. I waved my fingers and stuck out my tongue like you might do to get a small child to laugh. I can still see her standing there. She looked back at me, and smiled without a care in the world. She held Short Rib tight as the elevator doors closed.

The therapeutic fib I told my mom was that I would see her soon. But I also told her the truth when I said I had work to do. Once in my office, I reached out by phone and text to local business leaders to see how they were doing and what the Chamber could do to help. No one I spoke to feared the virus; it was the impact on their businesses, families and employees that scared them the most.

"Oh, we are taking a severe hit," a local hotelier said. "It's been nothing but cancellations today. I was in the hotel industry for 9/11 and it feels very much the same."

"We are shortening shifts, calling off staff and postponing any hiring," a restaurant owner shared. "I am examining my controllables in marketing, advertising, design, print, and other discretionary spending."

"We spent all day delaying shipments for March, April and May," a local retailer added. "We are trying to manage our expenses and use this opportunity to make us lean and mean."

"Speaking with lenders about lines of credits and delaying payments," another business owner advised. "We will be communicating with landlords as April first rents will be due and cash flow will be a challenge."

In Upstate New York, our local economy was shut down a few times every year by snow or ice storms. But never indefinitely because of a public health emergency. Everyone would be traumatized. The pandemic would test the resilience of every leader, government agency, business, family and individual.

The American Psychological Association defines resilience as: "The process of adapting well in the face of adversity, trauma, tragedy, threats or even sources of threats." Studies show that having at least one stable and committed relationship with a supportive caregiver, someone who loves you, is the key to becoming resilient.

For me, my resilience was emboldened by the support I had from everyone who worked with me at the Chamber. Collectively, our professional staff - - Kathleen, Sara, me, Denise, Richie, Andrea, Deb, Annamaria, Liz, and Devin - - worked at a chamber in one role or another for a combined 125 years. While none of us ever experienced a pandemic, we would do this together.

"We are all smart, resourceful and resilient," I said in an early morning text. "Let's figure out what we can do to help our community. I think we throw out the limitation of supporting just our members and help everyone."

Later that day, I sent an email to 10,000 people, everyone in our database. I wanted them to know we cared. In this email, I gave out my cell phone and encouraged everyone to call, text or email me if we could help. This was the best way I could think of to be sure they knew they too were not alone.

Tracy Shimkus Cheifetz
Mar 12, 2020

I am trying to remember these changes are temporary, but oh they are so frustrating and heartbreaking. I know the world is literally all dealing with these temporary changes and I am not alone, doesn't really make it easier. My Mom's nursing home is not accepting visitors. Our spring break trip to Orlando for baseball was cancelled. Tonight we get an email from the Superintendent of Schools that Fairfax County will still remain open at this time, but all Sports and other extra curriculars are cancelled until April 12th. This is BASEBALL season!!! Joel and Jared will not have in class college for at least the next three weeks and who knows if Jared's college graduation ceremony will take place. I know things could be worse. Believe me – I very much get that right now. I just needed to vent. Tonight Jason had an inter squad scrimmage. Then he had his chorus concert. I took lots of pic because I don't know when we will do either again. For other Westfield baseball people - will edit pics in my future free time. Lol.

    I didn't realize it at the time, but what a gift it was for the Wesley to give me that chance to see my mom in person, one more time. Tracy and Trisha didn't get that same opportunity, nor did millions of people around the world as we were told to isolate. To make it more frightening, none of us knew when we might see the people we loved again.

    "I sent a quick letter to mom with a picture in it due to the new restrictions," Trisha said to me in a note that accompanied a larger picture book she asked me to deliver to the Wesley. Joanie texted me to get my mom's address so she could send cards to my mom regularly. Joel and Jason sent Grammy Amy postcards about school and their extracurricular activities. A Wesley staff member produced a "Cartoon Dogs" sensory book because he knew how much she loved dogs. My mom saved all of these in a drawer in the dresser near her bed.

Tracy sent a lot of notes too, often with photos. "I'm so sad we can't travel to be with you today," she wrote early in the lockdown. "I hope you know how very much we love you and miss you. The world has gone a little crazy. We are all doing okay. Love you and miss you."

On March 13, 2020, the Saratoga Crew would also become a collective force for good. Darryl was an expert in the local hospitality sector. Ryan has a wealth of experience managing stage productions and facilities. Shelby was a leader in Saratoga's economic development for more than 15 years. No one had a better relationship with downtown businesses more than Deann. Samantha knew more about the history of Saratoga than anyone and understood what it took for Saratoga to make a comeback over these past fifty years.

Collectively, our six organizations had a professional staff of more than 50 people, one of the most comprehensive databases, and largest social followings in Saratoga. There was a short but proven track record of collaboration between us. As it turned out, we also left our egos at the door and did whatever it took to save Saratoga, no matter who got the credit.

When the six of us arrived at Wheatfields this Friday the 13th, the host gave each of us a hug. We sat close to each other at a table near the window still unaware of the risks this virus posed to everyone. I immediately shared that I heard from a lot of people who asked me what was happening at our local hospital, schools, food pantries, the unemployment office, and the small business administration, to name a few.

Ryan remembered when there was a blizzard in Buffalo and the local radio station became the place where people got local information. So I called Star Saratoga's owner from the table. They had an FM and AM station, and also streamed their broadcasts online, so everyone could listen no matter where they were. We offered to line up local experts for a Special COVID-19 broadcast on Monday morning, and the owner said yes. This was the first of many times when the Saratoga Crew took matters into our own hands but we were certainly not alone.

With schools shut down, teachers, like Lisa, also had to take matters into their own hands. For Lisa, teaching is a passion, not just a vocation. She spends hours differentiating her lessons (a process I'm still trying to understand), and she has invested her own money (and likely a lot of mine, too) into classroom furniture, supplies, learning materials and decorations. Every year her classroom is newly themed, color-coordinated, organized, fun and conducive to learning.

On the evening of March 13, the Principal of the St. Mary's School told everyone: "St. Mary's School will be closed from March 16 - 20th. Students have been sent home from school today with materials in preparation for the distance learning that will take place next week." The fact that their school sent students home with tablets was a big advantage over many public schools where this was not feasible.

That weekend, Lisa and her coworkers did their best to create virtual classrooms with little guidance and no training. The Saratoga Crew secured more than a dozen local experts to appear on our COVID-19 radio show. The Chamber's staff transformed our Restaurant Week scheduled to start March 20 into a Take Out Week. By the time our COVID radio show was on the air on Monday morning, Lisa somehow managed to start teaching her fifth graders virtually from our dining room while the students were at their own homes. We worked all weekend to make this happen.

"In times of crisis, we tend to see what people are made of," Governor Cuomo said as he spoke of his tremendous respect for healthcare professionals. In New York State and New York City, healthcare professionals were on the frontline of the fight to save people's lives against this virus. If my mom had still been a nurse, she would have been one of these heroes. Instead the heroes at the Wesley spent their weekend trying to figure out how to safely take care of her and all of the facility's residents in isolation.

THE WEEK OF MARCH 16, 2020

COVID-19 TRIED TO SEPARATE and divide us. I couldn't visit my mom, and Lisa couldn't be with her students. Katie couldn't work in the bookstore, and Ben couldn't audition or perform. In a matter of days, I would work from home as would every member of the Chamber's staff. The same was true for everyone in the Saratoga Crew and their employees. Even though we were isolated, I'm proud to say that all of us realized more quickly than most that we were Stronger Together.

"Collaboration is the key to our success here in Saratoga," read the subject line in the email I sent on Monday, March 16. In this email, we announced publicly that the six of us in the Saratoga Crew agreed to work together. "When you contact any one of us, we're all coming to help," I said in this email.

Around the world, 15,000 people had lost their lives to COVID-19. Schools and colleges were closed, and kids were now at home. Parents had to figure out how to care for them. There were food shortages in area supermarkets, and people were scared. We were being told what we couldn't do. No one knew what they should do.

Just a day earlier, I met at the Chamber offices with our VP of Finance, Deb Zeman. She and I had worked together since 2003. I hired her two weeks into my new job as President of the Adirondack Regional Chamber, in Glens Falls, New York. In our second week together, we had to scramble to make payroll - so we had experience dealing with a crisis. It took years, but Deb and I put that chamber back together financially. When I was hired as the President of the Saratoga Chamber, I asked Deb to come with me and she did.

Now, in 2020, we had to figure out how to save the Saratoga Chamber, our employees, and their families from potential financial ruin. What expenses could we cut? What reserves did we have available?

What did we need to do to have everyone work remotely? Everything was on the table that morning, including pay cuts and layoffs. Not everyone understood the seriousness of the situation.

"Why are the two of you in the office on Sunday?" another employee texted us. I responded: "My guess is that our membership revenue will decline precipitously. We can't sell our events. We can't ask our members who are closed to pay their memberships. Plus, we are leading the response to this pandemic for our community. We're trying to figure out how to make this work."

Lisa started her first virtual classroom on Monday, March 16; via Zoom and Google Classroom. The challenges multiplied almost immediately. Lisa was the school's Teacher of the Year, but she never taught a single class online. She had a Master's degree in Education. Yet she was never offered a class on teaching fifth grade virtually. No one ever dreamed of teaching elementary school children this way. Now it was the only option.

"If I have to do this next year, I will quit," Lisa said constantly. It wasn't that she couldn't teach this way. It was that this was not an appropriate or effective learning environment, particularly for younger children. She had been tasked with the impossible.

Learning from home, some students had more parental support than others, and not everyone had reliable internet connections.

Some students with special needs or learning disabilities needed more hands-on activities but this was impossible to do virtually. Lisa no longer controlled the learning environment, and this meant she was now in competition for her student's attention with other siblings, the television, video games, parents or caregivers and pets.

Lisa's dad, Richard, was an amazing carpenter. He's the one Lisa always called when we needed something fixed or she had an idea for a project. We always told him he was "super good." But every project took him longer than he expected because he wanted perfection; good enough wasn't acceptable.

Lisa is the same way, and she expects all of her students to excel. If just one of them did not, she took this personally. Teaching remotely drastically reduced how she could interact with students and evaluate their performance. The fact that so much of this was out of her control provided no consolation. Students were distracted and lost interest. She had parents who were unable to help. There were constant struggles with the software and the technology. Good enough wasn't acceptable to her. She wanted to be super good, just like her dad, but that was impossible in a pandemic.

Katie joined us in Saratoga on St. Patrick's Day. The day before this, Governor Cuomo ordered restaurants to close, except for take-out. Katie came to see Ben. "I do want to come home for a little bit. I haven't seen Ben since November. I was going to invite him to visit me in Boston but I'm not sure how great a plan that is."

At Katie's suggestion, I ordered corned beef and cabbage for take-out from one of our favorite local restaurants. The four of us gathered together at the dining room table. We had to move Lisa's computer and teaching materials from the table to use it. This was the first time in five days Lisa and I took a break from work.

We talked about the pandemic and the havoc it created for theaters, schools, bookstores and the local Saratoga economy. According to Katie, there was one silver lining. "When MIT said we had to increase social distancing, I thought to myself that I had prepared my whole life for this," she shared while laughing. "Me too," added Lisa.

Katie and Lisa prefer to spend time with a few friends or family members. Crowds of people are not their thing. In third grade, Katie was diagnosed with Asperger's Syndrome, now categorized as Autism Spectrum Disorder. Lisa often suggests she too is on the spectrum. For Katie and Lisa, the order to practice social distancing was a relief.

I on the other hand needed to interact with people; to network, talk and lead teams. Ben wanted to perform in front of people too. For me, it was entirely unnatural to not shake someone's hand when I met them. I also love to run. But now if someone walked toward me on the sidewalk, I veered onto the street to stay at least six feet away from them.

"If you were all vegan, the shortage of meat would not be an issue," Ben suggested. "I can always grow my own food if this gets really bad." We laughed about our different perspectives as this crisis unfolded. I don't think Lisa, Katie or Ben expected this Shimkus family reunion to last more than a week, so we enjoyed this time together.

I didn't dare tell them what I thought, not yet anyways. To me, the pandemic represented one of those times when families had to stay together. It was both a public health and economic crisis. No one was safe, and we could lose everything. For now, I kept this to myself. This was a moment to talk about the things that made us laugh, and thankfully we laughed a lot on St. Patrick's Day.

At 12 noon, on March 17, Tracy was the first to attempt a virtual visit with mom. The Wesley moved swiftly to attempt to set this up. It didn't work at first, but two hours later, Tracy texted me: "We talked to mom. She looks good. Doesn't seem to know what's going on. Only good part about the loss of memory is that she doesn't remember if we visited, or when we visited."

On Saturday, Lisa, Katie, Ben and I had our first virtual visit with my mom. Katie set up her laptop on the coffee table in our living room. Lisa and Katie sat on the couch. Ben and I stood behind them. Looking at the computer screen, my mom sat with Ribbie, not the new dog.

"Hi mom, it's Todd," I said as she appeared on the screen. "I'm here with Lisa, Katie and Ben." I said each of their names slowly and paused so they could wave and say hi to her themselves. "How's the puppy?" I asked her. She told us he had been out for a walk and played with the kids. "Did he bark at the kids," I asked. "No. He doesn't bark," she told us.

Virtual visits were limited to fifteen minutes, and the time came and went so fast. My mom was definitely alert and happy. It was difficult to tell whether she recognized any of us. We were all crowded onto the screen, and I think it was hard for her to follow who spoke as we all tried to chat. These visits were a way for us to check-in on her. They were not useful as a way for us to stay connected.

Nowhere was the panic greater than in New York City's hospitals as they became overrun with patients. Soon they would need to use refrigerated containers to store the dead bodies. President Trump would order the US Navy to send a hospital ship to New York City and the Army Corps of Engineers to build temporary hospitals in Central Park. Patients from New York City would be shipped to other hospitals, including Saratoga Hospital.

On Wednesday, March 18, the Governor directed non-essential businesses to implement "work from home" policies. Businesses that relied on an in-office workforce had to send 50% of their workers home. One day later, this changed and businesses now had to send 75% of their employees home. On Friday, 100% of the workforce was required to work from home.

Governor Cuomo declared that all "Non-essential gatherings of individuals of ANY size for ANY reason are canceled."

The shock of what this meant for Saratoga's economy was obvious when I walked downtown on Thursday. Our once vibrant downtown, always filled with people, cars, bikes, and dogs, was closed and nobody was there. "Not. One. Person. #surreal," I said in a post on Instagram with a photo of an empty Broadway.

As businesses closed, many had no choice but to lay-off their employees. I sent a text to the Saratoga Crew, "Local restaurants want us to put a page together on our websites to help their employees get information on the services available to them now that they are unemployed. Any suggestions on where to start?"

The Chamber staff frantically worked on the Saratoga County Take-Out Week campaign. Hearing from so many businesses in need of help, we defined take-out more broadly to include: local breweries, wineries, florists, clothing and jewelry stores, beauty salons, golf courses, fitness facilities, and anything else where you could purchase a product or gift card online for delivery or curbside pickup. The goal was to get these businesses as much cash as we legally and safely could so they survived what we thought was a temporary crisis.

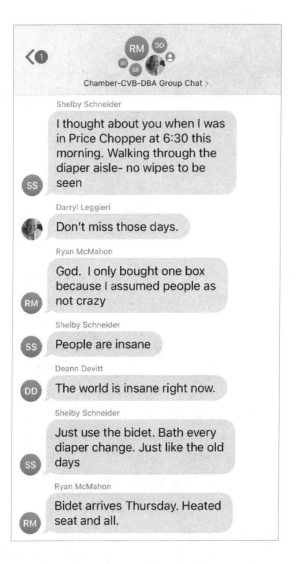

Nowhere was the panic more obvious than in the grocery stores. They were still open, and within days they were sold out of toilet paper, disinfecting cleaners and baby wipes. Deb Zeman texted me photos of empty grocery shelves at a big box store. "Seriously unnerving," she said. "No canned goods, pasta, frozen vegetables, eggs or meat just to name a few. Employee told me that I need to be there by 7 a.m. to get anything."

I had to see this for myself. Knowing Ryan had two young children, I hoped to score some baby wipes that I could give to him. I stopped at one supermarket and the aisles were barren; just as Deb had said. I stopped at a second store, and again there were no baby wipes or cleaning supplies. On one shelf, there was a small stock of toilet paper with signs that indicated each customer could purchase just one package of four rolls. I bought one just in case. Better safe than sorry.

As Governor Cuomo shut down our state this week, he declared that "essential services were exempt" and could remain open. If you were deemed essential, it was a golden ticket and those designated as such saw huge financial benefit. But if you were not, you had to close and no one said how long this might last.

At first, there was no list to define exactly what businesses were essential, and I received hundreds of emails, text messages and calls from business owners who wanted more information. Because I was accessible, I was forced to play the role of lawyer and business advisor. The rules assumed the government could treat every business the same, but I quickly understood from listening to their stories that each had a unique set of circumstances.

What does this special clause mean?

The Saratoga County Chamber has received a ton of calls, texts and emails asking us what this special clause to the right means.

Thanks to **D'Orazio Peterson LLP** and **Dowling Law PLLC**, here's what we know: "The Order is a bit ambiguous since the example used is an essential service. This is further complicated by the fact that there may be multiple offices/businesses in the same building each with one employee. We have been recommending that, in the absence of further guidance and given the potential for penalties, all employees should work from home if they can. This is most consistent with the social distancing the state is looking to accomplish.

Special clause in Governor's Guidance on Essential Services

"Any business that only has a single occupant/employee (i.e. gas station) has been deemed exempt and need not submit a request to be designated as an essential business."

If it's necessary to have someone onsite, consider limiting that onsite presence to what is necessary to accomplish the business purpose and ensure that practices of frequent cleaning/disinfecting and social distancing continues."

Click here to read the Governor's Guidance on Essential Services.

"Do you have the answer as to what category hotels fall into, essential versus non-essential," a local hotelier asked. A local retailer said; "We cannot just abandon our locations. They must be checked on regularly. But please have bond money in case I end up in jail."

On Friday, March 20, the state published a list of what the Governor deemed essential, and this included: media organizations, pharmacies, grocery stores, public transportation; hospitals, public safety and first responders, mail and delivery services. The Chamber emailed a link with this information as soon as it was released.

As business owners read the guidance provided by the Governor, they were desperate to find a loophole to be able to stay open. One owner asked me if I thought she could deliver her products to customers? Another asked if I thought they could stay open if they sold food?

Several asked me to interpret a clause in the guidance that read: "Any business that only has a single occupant/employee has been deemed exempt." A local guitar store owner, Matt McCabe, asked if I thought he could stay open because he'd be the only one at work? Another wanted to know if it was okay for her to go to work to pay her taxes?

We could not get clarification from any state officials about this clause and its true meaning. On Saturday, I saw a post from a local law firm that provided some insight, and they agreed to let the Chamber share their opinion. But even their interpretation came with a caveat: "The ORDER is a bit ambiguous," they said. "Consider limiting onsite presence to what is necessary to accomplish the business purpose."

Even in the best of times, the biggest challenge small businesses often face is lack of access to money. Now as they were forced to close, they might have zero revenue, and no one knew for how long. This was a huge threat, and I feared our local economy was headed for a disaster.

Lucky for me, I knew Steve Bulger, the Regional Director of the SBA, and I had his cell number from the time he was the Chair of the Saratoga County Republican Committee. I texted him a simple request; when the SBA has any information about support programs, please let me know right away.

That afternoon, he shared with me that the SBA was now authorized to accept applications through the Economic Injury Disaster Loan (EIDL) program. Normally used to help businesses recover after a natural disaster, like a Hurricane or earthquake, the SBA now planned to use the EIDL program to help businesses negatively impacted by COVID-19.

We emailed a link and information about the EIDL loan to everyone right away, and local SBA offices hosted virtual workshops on Zoom. There was one problem; more people wanted to participate in these online workshops than could be accommodated. People who were shut out were frustrated, but I came up with a solution.

Richie Snyder, the Chamber's Vice President for Communications, signed up for the next available EIDL workshop. We recorded this workshop using a laptop and a cell phone, and uploaded the video to the Chamber's social media channels, so that we could share it ourselves.

"This is going to be like a bootleg cassette of a rock concert in the 1980's," I said to him as we started the recording. Within one day of us sharing this video, 2,000 people watched it and had the information they needed to apply.

"Thank you Todd for all you are doing," the Mayor texted me on March 20. "I haven't had time to send a note but your work is amazing." Deann texted all of us: "Wow is all I can say. So much has changed. This freaking sucks. I'm ready for it to all be over." We did great work as the Mayor said. But Deann was right too, this week did suck.

By March 20, I had worked twelve straight days. There was an adrenaline rush to this work. I always believed my work at the Chamber was meaningful and had an impact. But now, I was being called upon to save the people and the community that I loved.

As this crisis unfolded, I became the most public figure in Saratoga and definitely the most quoted. We took over the radio station on Monday, and I said yes to every media interview request. We sent emails to thousands of people every day, including weekends. I was active on social media amplifying the information and ideas being shared by the chamber with my friends and followers.

To give people some hope, I agreed to write a column for a local newspaper. In this, I focused on how we had already demonstrated resilience in the first couple of weeks of this crisis, and how important it was for us to help one another. "There likely will be days where the trauma and tragedy is real, personal and hard to comprehend," I wrote. "We can climb any mountain. We can climb out of any hole too."

Two years later as I looked back on this column, I wanted to cry as I could see just how naive I was in those first days of the pandemic. The hole we were about to fall into was historically deep, and the trauma and tragedy we faced in our world, nation, state, and local community was unprecedented. While I was correct to suggest we help one another, I'm not sure we were ever united, and deep divisions with respect to our response to the pandemic would soon arise and were rarely resolved.

MARCH 23, 2020

HOPE WAS IN SHORT SUPPLY in this first full week of our shutdown. Everything was closed, and no one was supposed to gather together for any purpose. This is when we learned the true meaning of social distancing, and began to feel the effects of forced isolation.

"If you go outdoors to exercise, keep it to solitary activity," the Governor said. "And keep six feet of distance from others. We know the most effective way to reduce the spread of this virus is through social distancing and density reduction measures."

The only people allowed to venture out were those required to work. They were the EMTs that transported more and more sick people to hospitals, and nurses and doctors in a desperate search for ways to save lives. This included essential workers, the employees at the big box stores and the takeout cooks. We needed them to work so we had food to eat.

To keep workers safe, organizations everywhere tried to secure supplies of personal protection equipment (PPE) — masks, gloves, gowns, goggles, etc. There was an urgent and unprecedented global competition to secure these products. Every government, healthcare facility, nursing home, public safety department, and essential business was suddenly looking to purchase PPE.

Saratoga Hospital's President emailed me; "Would you be good with sending out a note to membership on the Hospital's behalf to ask if companies have any PPE they could lend or give us? I am okay with replacing it some day when things settle down." I got on the phone right away and called businesses I thought could help.

Within twenty-four hours, a local contractor delivered a case of masks. A local hardware distribution center donated gloves and masks, and a local bottling company did the same. We issued a community wide social media call for action. Shelby talked to local manufacturers and asked if they could quickly manufacture PPE.

Governor Cuomo led a search for more hospital capacity: "Today, we are traveling the state looking at locations for the Army Corps of Engineers to build new hospital beds. We are asking all New York State hospitals to increase capacity by one hundred percent. Every hospital must do its part to expand capacity."

Four days later, on March 25, the Department of Health ordered nursing homes to readmit residents who had been sent to hospitals with the coronavirus, as long as they were "medically stable." This action was taken to free up hospital beds, but it had tragic unintended consequences.

This directive was reversed in early May, as evidence suggested this policy led to COVID-19 outbreaks in nursing homes with many other residents dying as a result. The full extent of the death toll caused by this directive would be debated for years to come. Thankfully for my mom, not one staff member or resident at the Wesley tested positive for the virus during the first wave of the pandemic. This was quite the accomplishment, but unfortunately this would not last forever.

Just a few days later, Saratoga Hospital's President and I both received a generous offer. "We'd like to raise funds to provide meals to hospital workers on the front lines fighting the pandemic while supporting local restaurants at the same time," a group of local residents shared with us. "We see you are both on the front lines of communication and know the latest needs. We'd like to help."

The Chamber shared a list of restaurants we knew needed help and were doing takeout, and the Hospital President connected them with his team to organize the food deliveries. This effort was called FLAG Saratoga, and FLAG stood for Front Line Appreciation Group. They quickly raised more than $40,000 and purchased more than 5,000 meals from local restaurants. "Our staff are doing such good work," the President said in his response. "I see them every day just staying focused and doing their job. Anything that shows them the community notices this work is a good thing."

The financial struggle became real for even more people as the stock market crashed. The Dow plummeted thirty-seven percent in a couple of weeks. For comparison, the Dow fell forty-nine percent in 2008's Great Recession. But that decline took place over the span of a year and a half. The Dow dropped eighty-nine percent in the Great Depression, as that collapse took nearly three years to reach the bottom. The speed with which the market fell this time scared many of us.

In just a couple of weeks, everyone with a retirement account received a very troubling first-quarter statement. With about fifty percent of the Chamber's reserves in an investment account, I'd see this loss personally and professionally. This loss may have been on paper, but anyone that looked at these losses felt traumatized. The losses in lives, jobs, retirement accounts, paychecks, and businesses mounted while the virus spread. It wasn't just the stock market that crashed.

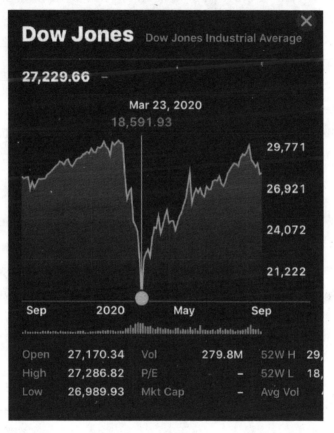

"Last year, you were so kind to meet with me after my layoff," a local resident emailed me. "Unfortunately, I am in a similar position again. I've tried filing for unemployment through the Department of Labor. The website keeps crashing. I imagine the system is overwhelmed."

Without warning, tens of thousands of people lost their jobs. They tried frantically to apply for unemployment, but the state's website was outdated and overwhelmed. Unable to complete the online application and with unemployment offices closed, these people were forced to attempt to call the state's labor department. The state did not have enough employees in their call centers either, so no one could reach anyone.

In early April, 400,000 people in New York filed for unemployment in just one week. Saratoga's unemployment rate went from 3.7 percent in March to 13.2 percent in April. In March, 4,500 Saratoga residents were unemployed, but this number tripled to 15,600 in April. At times, I felt like all of them called me to see if I could help them.

The Chamber staff called local companies that we thought might hire people to fill open positions. We posted information about those companies and links to their employment applications. Firms that had open jobs included the hospital and the Wesley, as well as other area health care and nursing home facilities. Local nonprofits that worked with disabled adults needed employees, as well as big box stores and their distribution centers. All of these firms were deemed essential, and for them to operate, they desperately needed more staff.

Ben tried to apply for unemployment and to find a local job. I connected him to the general managers at two local distribution companies because I knew they paid well. In early April, he started full-time at Target's local distribution facility, at what he called a survival job. But the reality was that we were all in survival mode.

The Small Business Administration's (SBA) website crashed too, overwhelmed by the sheer number of businesses that applied for an Economic Injury Disaster Loan (EIDL). "Todd, I've been working on our EIDL application on-line," a local business owner emailed me. "I hit the submit button yesterday, then the site crashed. I was told by the SBA to start the process all over, download all the forms, and upload them. I was just about in tears."

The frustration level among business owners and those now unemployed was high. Everyone felt paralyzed by the uncertainty and lack of information coming out of Washington and Albany. No one had a business plan on how to survive a pandemic.

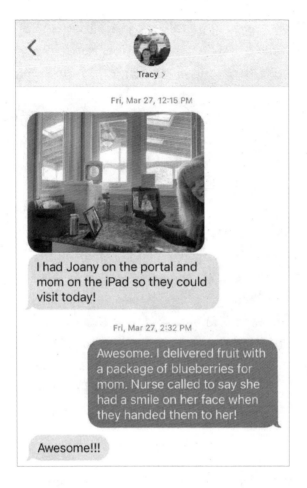

"I feel like I've become part lawyer, small business advisor and psychologist," I told Lisa one night. I took these calls every day, morning, noon and night. Because I often worked from home, Lisa, Katie and Ben heard what people shared with me and the raw emotion in their voices. Some people vented because they were angry, others talked about options, and a few cried as they feared the worst. The only thing I could do was listen and invite them to stay in touch with me.

"Isn't it awful about the virus?," Joanie texted me. "It's pretty scary. You almost don't want to go anywhere. I was in Walmart today. There were no Clorox wipes and no hand sanitizer. Any chance you can call on the Portal on Sunday so I can talk to Amy?"

The Wesley used Skype to host virtual visits. Because this was software my mom's sisters never used, they were unable to see and talk to her. Thankfully on March 27, Tracy engineered a workaround to fix this. She scheduled a Skype call with my mom on her iPad, and then started a Portal call with Joanie and Betty. She put both screens across from one another on her kitchen counter. Voila: my mom had a virtual visit with her sisters.

By now, the Wesley had also placed a table in the small area just outside the front door where family members could place items they wanted delivered to residents. Every Friday, I delivered a box of chocolate chip cookies for my mom and two fruit platters for the other residents on 2 Victoria. On the bag, I would write a note to my mom that told her that I loved her and hoped to see her soon.

Within one week of the lockdown, however, my mom experienced sporadic agitation and anxiety. She had trouble sleeping, and put her hands on other residents to assist them, but then became angry when they didn't listen. The staff was urged to give her a desk nursing task such as going through meal tickets instead of letting her do rounds, and the doctor prescribed Lorazepam to treat these symptoms.

By Friday, March 27, Ryan, Darryl, Deann, Samantha, Shelby and I had all worked nineteen straight days, and we needed a break. We talked and texted every day, and our organizations sent out daily emails to let everyone know what resources were available. Simultaneously, we tried to figure out how to save our own organizations and to care for our families.

"I know we cannot legally meet but I wish we could find a safe way to get together today," Samantha texted us that morning. Deann responded: "I'm so in need of social distanced human interaction." Ryan volunteered to host us at the City Center. Deann asked if we could meet outside on the roof? Ryan said yes, but advised that this involved climbing multiple ladders. It was now an adventure.

The sun shined brightly, and it was unseasonably warm. No one could see us on the roof of the city center. We felt liberated as we gathered here with each other.

Darryl and Ryan updated us on what they had done to reschedule events, conventions and meetings. "We haven't lost any business yet," they said. "Everyone is rescheduling. They still want to come to Saratoga. We'll be okay as soon as we can put the virus behind us."

Shelby and I shared information we gathered about local companies that were looking to hire. We talked about ways to support the Hospital's efforts to secure more personal protection equipment from local companies. Earlier in the day, Deann hosted a virtual meeting on Zoom with about thirty local retailers and she shared what they said.

At some point, we stopped this talk about our work and started to have fun. We joked and laughed together, and I could almost feel the stress, anxiety, and pressure to lead the community, the Chamber and my family melt away. This was the tipping point, where we went from being friendly colleagues to forever friends.

We made fun of how often Ryan swore, and how Darryl complained about sitting on the ground. We questioned how many cats Deann had. Shelby and Samantha took selfies with all of us. We promised we'd never show these photos to anyone, and declared that there was a "cone of silence" at these gatherings. Whatever we said was not to be disclosed to anyone.

We decided to meet every week in-person, at the City Center. Inside a large conference room that following Friday, Ryan set up six tables - - one for each of us - - so we were socially distanced. When we met, the conversation always began with the news of the week and what we thought we could do together, and they ended with jokes and laughter. As the Saratoga Crew worked to save our community, these meetings saved us.

APRIL 2020

The darkest days of the pandemic's first wave were upon us, in New York, by April 1, 2020.

More than 12,000 New York State residents were hospitalized with COVID-19. The health care workers in these facilities frantically tried to save the lives of as many patients as possible. One study suggested hospitalizations in New York alone could grow to between 55,000 and 110,000 in the next six weeks.

> **Andrew Cuomo** ✓ @NYGov... · 4/2/20 ⌄
> Every county in New York has now reported a Coronavirus case.
>
> This virus has marched across our state.
>
> We have counties with more cows than people. That didn't stop it.
>
> Urban, suburban, and rural: We're all affected.
>
> It will march across our nation next.
>
> 💬 261   🔁 2,066   ♡ 7,038   ↑

2,000 New Yorkers had already died from the virus. That number climbed at a staggering rate of more than 800 per day in early April. The virus had already killed more than 50,000 people across the world. Many, many, many more people in the US and the world would die.

We now understood that people could contract the virus without knowing it. Some never felt a thing: not a sniffle, cough, sore throat, headache or a fever. Others got it and died. It spread from person to person more easily where people gathered closely together.

Our capacity to test people for the virus remained limited, so tests were reserved for those who were symptomatic. As tests confirmed positive cases, those people were quarantined, and local public health officials traced and contacted everyone that person had been with in the last few days. These close contacts were required to quarantine too. At this point, the CDC recommended a two week quarantine for everyone who tested positive and those who had close contact with them.

More than a year later, we learned Governor Cuomo's family and friends were tested regularly. Officials with the state department of public health were sent to their homes to administer the tests. The tests were brought immediately to the state's lab for testing. Everyone that entered the White House was tested too. Within the general public, we didn't have this same luxury, so we never knew who had the virus until it was too late. That's why we were required to isolate and avoid close contact with everyone.

When they arrived in mid-March, Katie and Ben expected this family reunion to last just a few days. But as April arrived and the deaths climbed, Lisa knew I felt like they needed to stay with us. "If you don't think they should leave, you need to tell them," Lisa advised. "They'll listen if you explain what you know."

That night, I told Katie that there was no way MIT would continue to pay her if they couldn't reopen the bookstore. "Who will pay private school tuition if the economy collapses? This means mom could lose her job," I added. "Businesses are closed and the Chamber can't hold events, so I might have to lay people off and take a pay cut myself. The theaters are closed and we have no idea when Ben might be able to audition, never mind perform. There is also a virus out there killing tens of thousands of people, and we have no way to stop it. For now, the four of us need to stick together."

Like all of us, Katie and Ben wanted to know how long this might last, but it was impossible for me or anyone really to answer this question. So I suggested a compromise: "When it is safe and if you still have a job to pay rent, then I will drive you both back myself."

If we stayed together, Ben, Katie and Lisa decided we needed to perform. This was not something we had ever done before, but I suspected this idea was likely inspired as we all watched performers around the world take to social media to perform virtually.

For the Shimkus family music video, Ben selected the song, "You Will Be Found." This song was from "Dear Evan Hansen," and it was first performed by Ben Platt. It had a poignant message for this time which started with the song's first verse: "Have you ever felt like nobody was there? Have you ever felt forgotten in the middle of nowhere? Have you ever felt like you could disappear? Like you could fall, and no one would hear."

Ben sang that first verse by himself alone on camera. Katie, Lisa and I came into the video as Ben continued with the second verse, "Well, let that lonely feeling wash away. Maybe there's a reason to believe you'll be okay. Cause when you don't feel strong enough to stand. You can reach, reach out your hand."

Katie did a solo too, "There's a place where we don't have to feel unknown. And every time that you call out, you're a little less alone." We all sang the refrain together, "Even when the dark comes crashing through. When you need a friend to carry you, and when you're broken on the ground. You will be found."

With COVID-19, the dark came crashing through, and no doubt people felt lonely. Many called me for help, and just being accessible helped many to realize they were not alone. The one person who might have liked to see this video and to hear us sing this song more than anyone was mom, but there was no way for us to share it with her. When I did finally get to play this song for her, I played it over, and over again. It would comfort her when she literally was broken on the ground.

One week after our economy was shut down, President Trump signed into law the CARES Act which authorized the Federal government to spend more than two trillion dollars to help those adversely impacted by the pandemic. Most Americans received a one-time cash payment of $1,200. Those who qualified for unemployment were eligible for a $600 per week federal bonus through July.

For small businesses, the CARES act created the Paycheck Protection Program or PPP, a first-ever forgivable loan. Local banks would manage the PPP application process, which allowed the SBA to focus on a fix for its EIDL program. The money from the PPP had to be used as soon as the loan was received, mostly to retain or rehire employees.

If businesses followed the rules, the loan was forgiven and they didn't have to repay it. The President directed the agencies involved to put the rules in place so local banks could accept loan applications starting a week later, on Friday, April 3.

From the time it was announced, it was clear that every employer I knew planned to apply for a PPP. Even though Congress appropriated $350 billion dollars, it seemed likely to me that this money would be gone quickly. It was a race to get the money, and the Chamber's job was to give local employers a head start.

Every day, we emailed the latest information about PPP loans, and our email open rate tripled. We provided everyone with a list of local banks who told us they would accept PPP loan applications as well as a copy of the draft application. From these emails, local businesses learned what documents they needed to apply, who to talk with at their local bank, and the latest information on when the money might be available.

"At a time of uncertainty, one thing is certain. No other community leader in our region is maintaining the needed communication better or more frequently than you," a pillar of our business community said to me in an email.

With just hours to go until banks were required to accept applications, the SBA still hadn't published the rules. In a conference call with our local banks, Steve Bulger asked for patience and said, "Hey guys, it's like we are trying to fly a plane while building it."

Just a couple hours after the call, local banks got just enough information to proceed, and they didn't hesitate. The PPP program saved so many small businesses from ruin. Deann was one of the local bank employees who answered the call, and like her peers she worked crazy hours with no days off until the money ran out. We decided to make sure our local banks and their employees were thanked.

Lisa's first month of virtual teaching came to a close on Good Friday. It was school vacation week, and she needed some time off. Like her peers, she too worked seven days a week to create daily lessons that engaged her students in a virtual setting. This was never simple.

This week, we were supposed to fly to London, England, but traveling overseas was banned and we had to stay at home. Instead, Lisa set aside some time to work with Ben to plant several new gardens. Deliberations between the two of them also started as to what color to paint the exterior of our house. They planned to do this project themselves. I thought they were crazy.

Lisa also created a sign to thank essential workers in our community. She did this so that our home could be a part of the "518 Rainbow Hunt," a project modeled after a program in Italy. The local woman who started this campaign added the "518" because that is our area code. "I found that Italy was already displaying rainbows as a sign of unity," she said in a local interview. "It's just a good message and it's just helping people get through this crazy time."

Within a few weeks, the 518 Rainbow group had more than 100,000 members. Each posted photos of their rainbow creations and invited people to drive by to see them. There were driveway chalk rainbows, colorful ribbons tied around trees, rainbow light displays, hand drawn rainbow posters, and Lisa's rainbow "thank you" sign. The Chamber soon began to incorporate a rainbow heart in all our marketing campaigns as we sought to unify our community too.

By mid-April, it appeared the steps New York State took to slow the spread of the virus were working. "We believe we have hit the apex — and the apex is a plateau," Governor Cuomo said. "We're not out of the woods yet. We are still seeing new hospitalizations and new infections. Social distancing is working. We must keep it up."

While he offered a hopeful tone, the Governor extended the PAUSE another month, until May 15. He also imposed a first-ever mask mandate for everyone when in public, and directed employers to provide essential workers with cloth or surgical face masks. Not everyone agreed such a mandate was a good idea, preferring each individual had a choice as to whether to wear one or not.

For instance, President Trump said: "With the masks, it's going to be a voluntary thing. I'm choosing not to do it, but some people may want to do it and that's okay." My opinion was simple; there was certainly no risk to wearing a mask. So if there was even a small chance that wearing a mask might speed up the reopening of the Wesley and local businesses, I would do so without hesitation.

Even if you agreed to wear one, the challenge was where to get a mask. Because of the supply shortage for all personal protection equipment, the CDC posted a video online that showed people how to make your own mask at home. On April 16, Lisa watched this video and made one for me. The cloth came from a t-shirt, and she covered that with material from one of my New England Patriots ties to personalize my mask.

The next morning, I put my Patriots mask on in my car so I could legally walk into a local market. My glasses fogged up as soon as I entered the store. I moved my glasses up and down my nose, and tightened the mask, but nothing worked. Eventually, I took my glasses off and did my best to find what I needed so I could leave the store as soon as possible. Over time, I became more comfortable wearing a mask, but it never seemed natural.

By April 17, more than 3,500 PPP Loans were approved by our local banks for their local customers. More Saratoga businesses received PPP loans than in any of the other surrounding counties. Most were small businesses who received less than $150,000, but that was enough to save them for now.

In less than two weeks, the PPP monies provided by the Federal government were gone. We were right, it had been a sprint to get these funds. One bank president told me, "Todd, it seemed like the Chamber was the best source of information locally on the PPP program. Anyone that read the information you emailed had a head start on their application."

But we knew from our conversation with Deann that it was our local banks and their employees who did the real work to get so many applications filed so quickly. We decided to thank them and declared without any authority that this day was to be called; "Thank Our Local Banks Day."

To make this day a celebration, Shelby and I secured a large donation of Death Wish Coffee and cases of Oboys, a giant version of a pizza roll, both of which are produced by local companies. The Chamber printed thank you posters with the slogan, "Stronger Together." Each poster featured raised hands with shirt sleeves in a rainbow of colors. The posters, coffee and pizza rolls were packaged and delivered by the Saratoga Crew and several elected officials to dozens of local bank branches on this day.

Two more times in the next year, the Federal government would allocate even more funds for the PPP program. Each time, our local banks stepped up to help and the money ran out quicker than anyone expected. The Chamber, Discover Saratoga, Prosperity Partnership, and the Preservation Foundation would all get PPP loans, as the program was altered and expanded over time to help save charitable and not-for-profit organizations as well as small businesses.

By April 18th, my 53rd birthday, I had worked 41 straight days, so I decided to take this day off. Everyone that wanted to talk to me about masks, PPP loans, take-out, or our community's future had to wait. But it was hard to find a way to celebrate as most of my usual birthday activities were still banned.

Local golf courses initially allowed to open were now closed. My favorite coffee shop, restaurant, and brewery were closed as well. The National Basketball Association, Major League Baseball, and the Professional Golfers Association all suspended their seasons, so there were no live sporting events to watch. In New York, we were still not allowed to gather in groups so there was no party with family or friends.

But what I thought I would miss the most was my mom's annual performance of "Happy Birthday." Every year, she sang this song to her kids and grandchildren on our birthday. Sometimes it was in person, other times it was by phone. With Alzheimer's, Tracy always reminded her of our birthdays and helped her to keep this tradition alive.

I did the same in February for Joel on one of my visits. As she sang Happy Birthday to Joel, I filmed her as she held Ribbie and looked right at the camera. When she finished the song flawlessly, she added, "and have a wonderful day. I have to see you soon."

Now trapped in isolation, there was no way for anyone to guide her through this process, or so I thought. Early in the morning on my birthday, I got a notification on Facebook, and learned that Tracy, Lisa, Katie and Ben arranged for more than a dozen people to appear in a video to wish me a Happy Birthday. They left the best for last.

"Okay, go ahead," I heard Tracy say. My mom looked at the screen and started to sing. "Happy Birthday to you. Happy Birthday to you. Happy Birthday, Dear Todd. Happy Birthday to you." Tracy shouted, "Yeaa!!!," as my mom finished with a big smile on her face. Tracy was excited, she caught my mom on a good day where she remembered the words and said the correct name at the end. It was amazing but it wouldn't always be like this.

Two days later, on April 20, it was our turn to sing Happy Birthday to our mom. She was born on this day, in 1944, to Bernhardt "Benny" Wehkoja and his wife, Lillian. After Betty and Joanie, she was the third of the five Wehkoja children.

They were all raised in Worcester, Massachusetts, where my grandfather worked for a large manufacturer. My grandmother was a stay at home mom who never learned to drive a car. My grandfather called me, "Poika," which means boy in Finnish. To honor my grandfather, Lisa and I decided to name our son, Benjamin. Most called him Ben, but everyone in my mom's family called him Benny, just like my grandfather.

The Wehkoja family spent a lot of time together. Joanie and Betty were both bridesmaids at my mom's wedding. As kids, my mom took us to Joanie's house for Thanksgiving, while we all gathered at Betty and her husband, Jack's house, on Christmas Eve. Everyone in the family went to my grandparents for New Year's Day breakfast.

Because of the lockdown, not a single family member could be with my mom for her 76th birthday. The exact opposite was the case just one year earlier when she turned 75, and everyone traveled to Virginia to celebrate. For her 76th birthday, the best we could do was a virtual visit and invite everyone to join us.

This was the first-time we did a group virtual visit. The Wesley now had my Facebook Portal which made it easier for Joanie and Betty to join us. With all eleven of us on one screen, our faces appeared very small. It was hard for all of us to see each person and to follow who was talking, especially my mom.

We enjoyed singing Happy Birthday to her, but she didn't realize it was her birthday. No gifts were opened, and no birthday hugs were given. It just seemed impersonal, lame, and sad. It was better than a phone call, but that was a very low bar to cross. Overall, she got little enjoyment from this visit as best I could tell, and she likely forgot about it a few minutes after we all said we loved her and would see her soon.

Later that day, I wrote on Facebook: "It has been 39 days now since I have been able to see and hug my mom, Amy Shimkus. She is being incredibly well cared for by our friends at The Wesley. But today was her 76th birthday and no virtual chance to sing happy birthday is even close to what we all wanted. We all want our nation and its leaders to do everything they can so that my mom and all of us are safe again. No more politics. No more excuses. No more pointing fingers. We are 'Stronger Together' and my mom deserves nothing but your best!"

By the end of April, progress was made as hospitalizations and the number of deaths per day dropped considerably in New York. As a result, our Governor was portrayed as an early hero in the pandemic, and many suggested that our nation should follow his lead. His daily briefing remained popular, and now we all watched to learn how he planned to reopen our economy. He said the goal was to "build back better," but there was nothing in writing to explain what this meant.

The Governor said nothing about nursing homes, and as we expected my mom's situation had deteriorated during the lockdown. In mid-April, my mom complained of lower back pain, and told the nurse she fell. No one knew if this was true or not as there was no bruising or swelling. Her nurse told me they could not find anything wrong, so we agreed that the isolation likely had to be a contributing factor to her discomfort.

No one would do well in a situation like this, never mind someone with Alzheimer's. Most days now, my mom walked the floor of 2 Victoria with her dog in search of her kids. Other times, she was Nurse Amy doing rounds where she walked in and out of resident rooms to check up on them. She did all of this alone, as if we had abandoned her.

On May 1st when Tracy asked how she was doing, my mom shared that her side bothered her. She said this discomfort was caused by a "bumble stick." No one knew what this meant, not Tracy, me or the staff on the floor. My only salvation was that I thought the end of the isolation was near. The Governor said the PAUSE was set to end in two weeks, and I figured that once we started to reopen our economy that the same would be true of nursing homes. I just had to be patient or so I thought.

MAY 2020

THE SARATOGA CREW actually wrote a reopening plan for Saratoga's economy. One of the plan's pillars was for us to distribute PPE to local businesses. With a $10,000 grant just for this purpose, the Chamber purchased a large supply of disinfecting cleaner and spray bottles. At our request, two local distilleries switched from making vodka and gin to produce hand sanitizer, and for every bottle we purchased they gave us another for free.

Local firms agreed to give us tens of thousands of single-use masks, and two local distributors printed posters that businesses could display to remind customers to wear a mask and to stand six feet apart. Another local company offered us 1,000 five-gallon plastic buckets, and a local hardware store gave us $50 gift cards.

All of these items were delivered to the City Center, and placed in the room where we continued to meet on Fridays. During our meetings, we put each of these items in the buckets and we began to call them "reopening kits." As local businesses were allowed to reopen, a member of the Saratoga Crew or one of our staff members personally delivered a kit to each owner to help them do so safely.

Our reopening plan also included a campaign to inspire our community to unite in the face of this trauma under the slogan, Stronger Together. We mass produced these Stronger Together posters and distributed them everywhere, and eventually they became visible on doors and windows at businesses across Saratoga. T-shirts with the logo were produced and sold, and businesses ordered masks for their employees with the logo. One local bank put out lawn signs with the logo at all of their branches.

"This sounds super cheesy but...I'm so proud of the work we're doing together. Thank you for letting me be part of this really cool, collaborative team," Shelby texted the crew.

TODD SHIMKUS

SARATOGACOUNTYCHAMBER
Posts

STRONGER TOGETHER — Stillwater
STRONGER TOGETHER — Waterford
STRONGER TOGETHER — South Glens Falls
STRONGER TOGETHER — Schuylerville

STRONGER TOGETHER
Saratoga County

STRONGER TOGETHER — Malta
STRONGER TOGETHER — Mechanicville
STRONGER TOGETHER — Round Lake
STRONGER TOGETHER — Clifton Park

View Insights   Promote

  Liked by **richiesnyder** and **52 others**

saratogacountychamber Have you downloaded your Stronger Together poster? .
👉 Click the link in our bio to find your communities poster! 🖤💕

bitemeshowny Yes!

savingfacebarbershop @jcregan4 we have to get one of the shop!

May 1, 2020

We did not distribute reopening kits to local schools. That's because Governor Cuomo never allowed them to reopen in the spring of 2020. "This is the best course of action to keep students, educators and staff safe," he tweeted. This meant Lisa, like all New York teachers, finished this school year teaching virtually. As she did this, her students struggled more and fell further behind every day, even the best of them.

One student consistently sent Lisa questions and homework after 8:00 p.m. As she investigated why this was the case she learned that the family owned a local restaurant that was open for take-out. The student spent her day at the restaurant instead of being at home alone, and she often helped out taking orders. That's why she emailed Lisa late at night because that's when she had time to do her homework.

We were so impressed by this story of resilience that Lisa and I placed a take-out order at this restaurant the next day. As we walked in, this student and Lisa were so excited to see each other and standing at least six feet apart they talked so long the pizza got cold. When we went to leave, her mom didn't want us to pay, and argued with us as we tried. Eventually, I dropped cash on a table, and Lisa and I ran out the door.

According to Tracy, our Mother's Day celebration with our mom was day 60 of our separation from her. Even this celebration was delayed one day because the Wesley didn't offer virtual visits on Sundays. Besides those who were in complete isolation, no one took more precautions than Tracy and her family to stay safe and virus-free.

One day, they ordered pizza and had it delivered. They directed the delivery person to leave the pizza boxes outside their house. Tracy went out to open them and moved the actual pizzas to cookie sheets. The boxes went straight into their recycling bin, and Tracy washed her hands before she touched anything. "It was almost easier to cook," she commented on Facebook.

Her husband, Craig, was a doctor on the front-lines at a hospital in Virginia. Every day when he came home from work, he stripped down in the front foyer, threw his clothes in the washer, and went directly into the shower. No one greeted him until after he was showered and dressed.

> **Tracy Shimkus Cheifetz**
> May 11, 2020
>
> Day 60 of social distancing – today we were able to have a portal party with my Mom to wish her a happy Mother's Day. Got to see Jared on the call too. 😊 In other news, Joel's internship with The Conrad Hotel in Washington DC is definitely not happening anymore. Last week, the pool company that manages most of the neighborhood pools, called Joel and asked if by chance his plans for this summer had changed. Since they had, he is now the manager of the Sully Pool. He went over there today and started figuring out what needs to be done to open the pool if the State allows it. This was the first time that Joel really left the house (other than to play catch with Jason). Crazy! Finally, according to my FitBit, I only walked 43 miles last week. I think I have ruined my feet, or I have old lady feet. Ugh. Not sure I can keep this up much longer. Lol.
>
>

No doubt Craig was at-risk, but none of them ever got sick or contracted the virus during this first-wave. The same was true for my mom and all of the residents and staff at the Wesley, as they too had ZERO positive cases. Elsewhere in New York, the Governor's office reported that 9,000 nursing home residents had tragically died from the virus in these first two months. This sounded bad enough, but the real extent of this tragedy was concealed until January of 2021.

Our virtual Mother's Day visit on the portal was similar to our virtual birthday party for her. With so many of us on the screen, our images were too small for my mom to recognize us. She was again confused as she tried to follow who was talking, and she had no idea it was even Mother's Day.

In a post on Facebook, Trisha spoke about our collective hope that the steps we took to protect ourselves from the virus would allow us to be reunited soon. "She gave up so much for me. Happy Mother's Day to my mom. I miss you mom. I will be there soon to hug you."

On Mother's Day, I got a text from the County Administrator, Spencer Hellwig, who asked me to help Saratoga County develop its own reopening committee. I said yes, of course, and was later named the committee's Vice Chair. When I shared this with Richie Snyder, he said; "They asked you to be Vice Chair because they know you'll do most of the work."

The committee met on Friday, May 15, in person, with all nine members plus a half dozen of the county's administrative leaders. We were required to wear masks and sit at least six feet away from each other. It was the first real meeting I had attended in two months, and doing so made it feel like we turned a corner. I delivered reopening kits to the county leaders, and the committee established a task force to create a reopening website where the county would share how it planned to help local businesses.

But Saratoga's reopening status was already in turmoil. Earlier that day, Governor Cuomo announced that just a handful of New York's 64 counties could start to reopen, and Saratoga was not one of them. No one at this meeting understood this decision, and the Governor's office refused to give us any explanation.

Since the first positive case in early March, Saratoga had fewer than 400 residents out of a population of 230,000 that ever tested positive. The highest number of residents admitted to the hospital on any one day was 15, but some were from New York City. On this very day, there was just one local resident in the hospital with COVID-19.

I didn't say anything publicly, but I sent an email to one of the Governor's top advisors who I had worked with recently since his office was in Saratoga. "We're getting crushed with questions and no answers," I wrote. "Seems like total BS that Saratoga is being left behind. Science does NOT tell us in Saratoga that we need to be caged and controlled. Our health care experts tell me we've stopped the spread here."

A few hours later, he replied: "I understand the frustration. Let's not forget where we started. Your school district was so freaked out they closed for the rest of the year in March before the state acted. So did Skidmore College. You had among the first positive cases in Saratoga. We have guidance. It's not perfect. We will keep working together and figure it out."

The trouble was the state was not working together with local officials and never really did. As long as Cuomo was Governor, everyone had to wait for what he said and then comply. That weekend, local officials from Saratoga and other area counties banded together and asked pointed questions about the data the state used to make these decisions. No one ever admitted the state used the wrong data, but on May 19 without any prior guidance the Governor finally approved Saratoga's limited reopening.

In phase one, local retailers could only reopen for curbside pickup. Then if there were no spikes in cases, these local stores could open fully two weeks later, in phase two. So as we saw it, the sooner we started phase one the sooner we'd get to phase two. That's when local salons and barber shops could reopen (and man did I need a haircut by now). Two weeks after that, phase three was set to begin and that's when we were told that local restaurants could reopen.

Unfortunately, not everything was on the Governor's reopening schedule. The Saratoga Casino, City Center, bowling alleys, and movie theaters were not given a scheduled reopening date. Fitness related businesses were initially told they'd be in phase two. Then suddenly, they were dropped from phase two and were not listed to be reopened in any of the four initial phases.

In media interviews and on Twitter, I suggested it would be possible to safely open SPAC and the Saratoga Race Course because they featured outdoor venues with lots of space to stay socially distanced. I urged state officials to work with local health departments to design a reopening plan for these facilities much as they did with beaches and state parks. There, they painted circles on the grass or required groups to sit at least six feet apart, and this allowed thousands of people to safely gather there. This idea sounded like a good plan to me, but eventually I'd have to adjust my expectations as would everyone in Saratoga.

There was also no guidance about when the state's nursing home visitation protocols might be changed. But again, I watched as the Wesley put up tents, and I assumed that this was for outdoor visits.

As I waited for this policy to change, a television reporter contacted me about a story they planned to do about the Wesley and their virtual visits. They wanted me to comment, and so I decided to connect them with Tracy too.

On May 25, our interview was the lead story. Tracy spoke about how concerned she was that by the time we might be reunited with our mom that she might forget who we were. I used this interview to send a message of kindness to those who now cared for our mom.

"The good news is that we know she is being incredibly well cared for by the heroes at the Wesley," I told the reporter and everyone who watched this story.

Tracy gave the reporter photos of our mom, from before she became a Wesley resident and a couple she took during virtual visits. The CEO of the Wesley described my mom as "spunky," and said the staff enjoyed Nurse Amy being with them. There was just one problem; there was no mention of Trisha.

Even though Trisha would not see this story where she lived, I knew she'd eventually see it on social media. So I texted her right after I watched the story and told her that Tracy and I talked about her and sent photos of her and our mom. I assured her that we tried to include her, but those quotes and pictures didn't make it into the final cut. I don't think she heard anything I said. She just knew she was left out.

Early the next morning, the Wesley shared the News 10 story on Facebook. Trisha suggested in a comment that the Wesley should have included her in the interview. I didn't want the Wesley mixed up in our family drama, so I asked Trisha to delete the comment. She did this, but on her own page she wrote: "What an incredibly huge let down from those in my life. Does anyone truly care about my feelings?" We did not talk for the next few weeks.

The top news story later that night came from Minneapolis, where four police officers killed George Floyd, a 46-year-old black man. This killing inspired marches and protests, including several over the next few weeks, in Saratoga. Here, local protesters renewed calls for an investigation into the 2013 death of Darryl Mount.

Darryl Mount was a 21-year old black man who assaulted his girlfriend outside of a bar in Saratoga. In his attempt to run from police, he fell from construction scaffolding, and later died from these injuries. While the police chief at that time said an investigation was underway, years later he admitted this was not true.

After one rally in Congress Park in late-summer, a protest leader walked to Phila Street where several restaurants had outdoor patios filled with patrons. "Yo. Yo. Yo. Listen," she yelled into a megaphone. "You know why we stopped? Because you all are really fucking comfortable out here having dinner. You are enjoying your lives as if the world just goes on. Darryl Mount is dead. The Saratoga Police killed Darryl Mount because he's a black man."

In response, city leaders announced that protesters who closed streets or disrupted business operations would be arrested if it happened again. This conflict between city leaders and protesters continued far longer than anyone expected, just like the pandemic. Both simultaneously created division in communities all over the U.S., and right here in Saratoga.

On the other end of the spectrum, the Shimkus family was united. During this first wave, no one was a better model of the Stronger Together theme than Katie, Ben, Lisa and me. We spent 78 straight days together in our small home in Saratoga, and somehow managed to survive.

Per our agreement however, Katie was allowed to go back to Boston on May 31. That's because she was still employed by MIT and the spread of COVID-19 had slowed considerably there. Ben wanted to leave as well, but Brooklyn was still a hot spot with a high rate of infection. Theaters were still closed and there were no auditions scheduled. There were few survival jobs in Brooklyn, so he stayed with us and continued to work at Target.

This was the longest time the four of us had lived together since Katie went to Emerson College in 2008. Our family's go-to place was our front porch. There, we watched other people walk, bike, run and drive by, and this made it feel like we were still part of a community. We read books, listened to music, petted Sammi, watched videos, enjoyed a cup of coffee in the morning or a beer after work. We talked about what to eat and where to get it; our jobs; our hopes and what we'd like to do after the pandemic; how my mom was doing; and news of the day.

These times on the porch gave me a chance to relax, to have some fun, to focus less on trying to save the world, and more on spending time in the company of the people I loved. I'm not sure Lisa, Katie and Ben will ever fully understand how incredibly helpful this was for me. Because we were together, I didn't have to worry about each of them, as I knew they were taking care of one another. This made me more resilient and freed me up to lead my community, to advocate for my mom, and to have some fun.

JUNE 2020

By June 1, six million people around the world had contracted COVID-19. Nearly 400,000 died. The United States had the most deaths with just over 100,000 having perished so far. With 24,000 deaths total, New York had the most deaths of any state. But it appeared, at least from a health perspective, that the worst was behind us.

With every day that passed, however, it became less and less likely that the Governor would allow the Casino, SPAC, Live Nation, and the Track to reopen. The anxiety level among Saratoga's business owners was at an all time high. No one was sure if local customers or visitors would return. In a show of solidarity, Deann organized a photoshoot and every business owner was urged to wear a Stronger Together t-shirt. I had a different idea.

In March when I worked from home, Lisa overheard one of our Chamber staff meetings on Zoom. Someone suggested we get a blow up horse costume. "Maybe Todd can wear it on opening day at the Track," they joked. After she heard this, Lisa went online and bought two. Rather than wearing a t-shirt, I figured a picture from Saratoga needed a horse and everyone needed a laugh.

Lisa helped me get into this costume and followed me as I walked out of our front door onto the porch. She took a short video of me "going to work" as I began to walk down the street. After she shared this video on social media, a friend commented; "That just made my day." Another friend added; "Thank God no one's lost their dignity during this crisis." Lisa responded to everyone: "I still laugh every time I watch this."

"Together, we flattened the curve," the Governor declared on June 3, 2020. "We changed the course of this virus and we did it by stand-

ing together." He was so excited by this progress that he announced restaurants could open for outdoor dining the next day.

This sounded like great news, and it would have been except that not all restaurants in Saratoga had outdoor dining space available. One local restaurant shared with me that with the limited space they had and social distancing rules that they could only accommodate 4 tables inside and just 16 customers at one time. "We need to have the capacity to serve more people or we will be out of business," she told me.

The Saratoga Crew wanted the city to approve the use of space on sidewalks, streets, parking lots, in parks, and alleys to dramatically

expand outdoor dining. We paid a local attorney to draft a resolution that we shared with city leaders. Before this announcement, we thought we had two more weeks to work this out, and now the need was immediate and local restaurants counted on us to get this done.

One way to encourage city leaders to act favorably was for me to speak out publicly. I did just this when I was interviewed by the Times Union. The reporter, who wrote a local restaurant blog, singled me out for this story because he was impressed with our Take Out promotion.

"Your promotion was bigger and better than any other I saw," he said. "I was impressed with how quickly you were able to start and how many restaurants participated." He promised to ask me a question about our desire to expand outdoor dining. But his questions also gave me a chance to talk about what we endured and what I thought the future held for Saratoga.

In response to his first question about the initial mood of the business community when the shutdown was imposed, I said: "At the time everybody understood the importance of trying to stop the spread of the virus. We thought it might be three weeks. I don't think any of us expected we'd be in June, still waiting to reopen."

He asked me when I thought Saratoga might get back to normal, and I told him I thought it might take 18 months. This meant our immediate challenge was to do everything possible to save our local small businesses so they could thrive again in 2021. For local restaurants, this meant we needed the city to approve an ordinance to maximize the flexibility for restaurants to use public spaces adjacent to their property for expanded outdoor dining.

In early June, Saratoga Living magazine released an article in which they called me a "Power Player." "Shimkus took early action during the COVID 19 crisis — and it paid dividends for Saratoga," they said. "The Chamber has been a veritable breaking news outlet, keeping the community updated regularly and sending out daily e-newsletters."

In response to this praise, I said triumphantly: "The six of us (in the Saratoga Crew) have finally been able to transition away from responding to the crisis — and all the trauma created by it — and to move on to talking about restarting the local economy."

In the City, we worked on expanded outdoor dining. At the county level, I worked with the members of the reopening committee to get $50,000 for a new advertising campaign to attract visitors back to Saratoga. Both items were scheduled for a vote on June 16, neither was guaranteed approval.

"I'm not supporting this expenditure to create a slush fund for the Chamber," one of the County's elected Supervisors said in an article even before we submitted our proposal. There was no slush fund. In fact, I pledged that we'd spend every dime contributed by the County on advertising.

To win county support for the campaign, there were two elected officials I considered swing votes. At my request, local hotels and restaurants reached out by phone and email to urge these supervisors to vote yes. Three of the Chamber's volunteer Directors also came to testify in support of our funding request.

In a stroke of parliamentary genius, the county officials who opposed this request suggested this money would be better spent on an expanded COVID-19 testing program; because no one could argue against more testing. The debate over this amendment was heated and lasted more than an hour. Eventually, the county attorney advised the Chair that he had the sole discretion to decide if this amendment could even be considered.

The chair then immediately ruled the amendment was out of order and called for a roll call vote. Just one of the two leaders we lobbied voted yes, so I thought we lost. But the clerk announced it passed. That was because one of the officials we thought would vote no thought they were voting for more testing and said yes. This made our victory pure luck, not the work of a power player.

Later that day, we did not need any luck to get the City to change its outdoor dining regulations. Here, it was a straight up power play. The primary objections to this change came from the Public Safety Department.

On a phone call, Commissioner Dalton told Darryl that she had issues with public spaces, especially roads, being used for outdoor dining. "What if there were a fire?," she asked. "How could we be sure there would not be any accidents?" They had a nice conversation, but no progress was made to change her mind.

An hour after Darryl's conversation, I sent Commissioner Dalton a more direct request: "I am going to take the city to task for NOT talking or working with the private sector to allow for use of adjacent public spaces in the same ways as all surrounding communities. Sad really. Why is this?"

A few days after this text, Mark Mulholland did a story that featured how two other towns had already allowed their restaurants to use public spaces to expand their dining capacity. The Commissioner of Accounts, John Franck, appeared at the end and urged the other Commissioners to support our local restaurants too.

On Tuesday, June 16, the Council voted unanimously to approve a new ordinance similar to the one we submitted. Commissioner Franck publicly thanked Ryan, Darryl, Deann and me for the work we did on the resolution. After the vote, I texted everyone: "We need to help the folks on Henry Street test this ASAP." Somehow I knew we won the battle but not the war.

On Saturday, June 6, Saratoga County public health officials confirmed the death of a 62-year old male from COVID-19. He was the seventeenth Saratoga resident to die from the virus. He would be the last person to die in Saratoga from this virus from this day until October.

In Saratoga, the next five months would be the most COVID-free of the pandemic. Here and now it was a uniquely safe time to be reunited with our loved ones. As businesses reopened, I should have been allowed to visit my mom, even if such visits were outdoors. The Wesley had already set up tents for this purpose, and the local COVID-19 data told us the virus had waned here.

This was when state protocols should have changed or local health departments should have been able to intervene. In the summer of 2020, our focus in Saratoga should have been allowed to shift to support the mental health of nursing home residents by reconnecting them with loved ones. But sadly, the pleas of family members were ignored by Governor Cuomo and tens of thousands of residents, the ones who survived so far, continued to decline as their caregivers remained locked out.

Saratoga County Office of Emergency Management
Jun 6, 2020

UPDATE: COVID-19 Information for Saratoga County
June 6, 2020

Ballston Spa, NY — The Saratoga County Department of Public Health Services today announced the most current stats* on COVID-19 in Saratoga County.

Confirmed cases of COVID-19: 502
Deaths: 17
Hospitalizations: 4

The Department also confirmed the death of one more county resident from COVID-19 — a 62-year-old male from Saratoga Springs.

The signs of my mom's decline were more and more obvious. Two months earlier, my mom sang Happy Birthday to me on video and it was perfect. Now Tracy tried to get her to do the same for Joanie and it didn't go as well.

"Mom sang but forgot who she was singing to," Tracy shared with me. "She said - happy birthday to guess who. Then she says it's for Joel. She tried again. This time, she sings - happy birthday Joanie you're not here though. She then wanted to sing happy birthday to Joel again."

On Friday, June 19, Saratoga was in the third stage of our phased-in reopening. To celebrate, the Chamber, the Saratoga Crew, and the Reopening Committee co-hosted Saratoga's largest ribbon cutting ever. At locations across Saratoga County, local businesses, elected officials and residents gathered to cut a piece of ribbon that featured the Stronger Together logo. We all did this at exactly 11:30 a.m.

"Twenty-seven communities in Saratoga County took part in the largest ribbon cutting ever held there," declared a reporter from News Channel 13. "It's to welcome the reopening of businesses as Covid loses its grip here in the region and New York State. Normally a ribbon is cut for one business. Officials say today's was a celebration of the reopening of all local businesses and the hopeful rebound in the economy."

No one from the Wesley attended these reopening ribbon cuttings. New guidance from the Governor's office on nursing home visitation didn't arrive until July 10. This meant the closest I could get to my mom in June was by participating in the Wesley's "Share a Step for Seniors" fundraiser.

Traditionally, this involved a walk around the Wesley campus with residents and their families. Now it was virtual, and family members, like me, signed up to walk or run a certain number of miles between June 19 and June 26. I pledged to run 18 miles, and I pledged that each of my runs would take me somewhere on the Wesley campus.

On the final day, I ran to a little park on the Wesley's campus and took a photo for a social media post. The Victoria Building where my mom lived was in the background of the photo, and I realized that if my mom looked out the window she might see me. I thought about waving my arms and hands just in case. Instead, I patted my heart twice with my right hand and pointed up to the second floor. "Someone please tell my mom that I will be back later," I posted that day.

After that final run, I went to work on the steps of City Hall. In the two weeks since the City approved expanded outdoor dining, local restaurants on Henry Street applied twice to use space on the sidewalk and street adjacent to their restaurants. The committee established to review these requests turned them down each time. My patience reached its limit, and I decided to use my status as a visible and vocal advocate to get action.

"I plan to be at City Hall tomorrow morning," I announced in a Facebook post on Thursday night, June 25th. "I am going to stay there until we get an approval for Henry Street Taproom, Scallions, Flatbread Social and Saratoga Paint and Sip Studio to use more of the sidewalk and street to expand outdoor seating. We've been talking about this for weeks. No more excuses! Stay tuned as I might need food and water if this goes on too long."

When I arrived at 8:30 a.m, the doors were locked per the City's COVID-19 protocols. So my protest started on the front steps, where Ryan, Darryl, and the Commissioner of Accounts came to support me. "I want you to know that my representative on the committee supports this application," Commissioner Franck told us. Local restaurant owners stopped to see me, and two television stations did interviews. Commissioner Dalton posted a meme on Facebook that declared my protest a "temper tantrum from a middle aged man" and a "lame publicity stunt."

The Mayor told me that she supported this request and her representative on the committee did too. I texted the Deputy Director for Public Works who I learned was on vacation. He graciously called me back and indicated that if the permit was just for using the parking spaces and sidewalk that he too was a yes. With three out of four committed to vote yes, Darryl reached out to Commissioner Dalton to make it clear that we preferred the committee vote unanimously. At 2 p.m. the committee met and the Henry Street application was finally approved.

We later helped restaurants on other streets do the same thing. Samantha and Darryl worked with the Public Works Commissioner to install picnic tables in Congress Park. We watched all summer as these outdoor tables filled up, and eventually as this use became so popular that it was extended permanently.

After summer ended, one of the owners of a Henry Street restaurant told us, "The outdoor patio is what saved our business. We would have been forced to close were it not for that space." Our work to save our locals and to bring our community together soon gained national attention.

On Tuesday, June 30, a story about Saratoga's pandemic experience appeared in USA Today. By now, SPAC had announced the cancellation of its entire summer classical program and Live Nation did the same with its concerts. The Governor allowed the Saratoga Race Course to open for horse racing, but no fans could attend, and the Saratoga Casino remained closed indefinitely.

SPAC and Live Nation entertained more than 500,000 people in 2019. More than 1 million people visited the race course in 2019, and another 1.6 million went to the Casino that year. This summer, none of these key drivers of our hospitality economy were open for business.

> **Unshackle Upstate**
> @UnshackleNY
>
> This story from @gsilvarole gives an extraordinary look into how @SaratogaChamber and small businesses in Saratoga have dealt with the impacts of COVID-19.
>
> Reopening NY: Saratoga Springs races to help struggling businesses amid COVID-19
> lohud.com

Knowing the devastation this loss might cause, the reporter was charged to write about how COVID-19 impacted Saratoga. Richie and I introduced her to the owner of a local Mexican restaurant, and he told her that locals who purchased gift cards in the early days of the pandemic made a big difference. He also added ominously, "but if this comes around with a new wave - I really don't know what to think."

A local hotelier told her that back in March bookings for this summer were wonderful, and they expected a busy season. "The cancellations that came were extraordinary," she added. The hotel closed for five weeks, furloughed staff, reconfigured their check-in process, and changed how they'd clean and sanitize everything.

But what stood out to me and made me smile was what the reporter observed and wrote herself: "In the midst of the pandemic, the Saratoga community has taken on the mantra: Stronger Together. Signs emblazoned with the phrase are everywhere - in store windows and in front yards and in the grassy berms of busy intersections."

SUMMER 2020

ON JULY 4TH, thousands gathered at beaches on Cape Cod, the Jersey Shore, and just to our north, in Lake George. But in Saratoga, the Firecracker 4 road race was forced to go virtual. There was no concert or fireworks in Congress Park, and no US Citizenship ceremony outdoors in the Saratoga National Historical Park.

In April, the demand for hotel rooms fell eighty percent. It was down seventy percent in May and sixty percent in June versus the prior year. We needed a strong summer for our hospitality sector to survive, and we had substantial evidence to suggest people wanted to come here.

But unfortunately, there was no consultation by state officials with local public health officials or the county's reopening committee. No variation in policies from one region to the next, no matter the local COVID case count. The Governor never gave our public health department a chance to develop local protocols that might have allowed a limited number of visitors to go to our outdoor venues.

"People come to Saratoga to gather in crowds," Ken Rotundo, the local owner of a market research firm, shared with us in early July. "SPAC is a gathering of a crowd, same with the Track; and people are in and out of our bars and restaurants. We've trained all these people to say don't do that. Now, we need to know what's going to bring them back?"

His firm surveyed 3,000 people who had previously visited Saratoga. Seventy one percent of the respondents were "very likely" to come back in the next six months. Eighty six percent said they were likely to visit when all COVID-19 restrictions were lifted. The respondents indicated a strong preference for outdoor events and for local employees to wear masks.

Using this data, the Chamber's summer tourism ad campaign featured our lakes, parks, trails, vibrant downtown, historical attractions and outdoor patios. We invited people to come and "Feel the Freedom." The trouble was there was little freedom to do what we really wanted to do this summer in Saratoga.

"We understand how trying it has been for New Yorkers not to see their loved ones and the challenges they've had to endure during this unprecedented pandemic," New York's Health Commissioner said in early July. But these words of compassion did little to reunite nursing home residents with loved ones. Instead, the new visitation protocols included stringent provisions that ultimately prevented in-person visits even outdoors.

Specifically, New York's protocols prohibited all visits for at least 28 days if any staff member or resident tested positive. This was double the Federal government's recommendation of 14 days. If even one employee tested positive, the entire campus was locked down. It didn't matter if the employee had contact with residents or not. Nor did it matter where or in what building on the campus this person lived or worked.

As July began, the Wesley still had no positive tests and so they set up tents and an online scheduling tool for families to use to book an in-person visit outdoors. Visitors had to show a negative test within seven days of the visit. I got tested and scheduled a visit with my mom, and a day later came a text from the Wesley that indicated one staff member had tested positive. This employee had no resident contact and did not work in the Victoria building. But New York forced the Wesley to cancel all visits for the next 28 days.

The best they could do was to set up window visits, and I scheduled my first one for Wednesday, July 22. I would get 20 minutes to stand on one side of a window while my mom sat on the other. To Tracy, this extended isolation from our mom took on new significance this week as she dealt with the death of her mother in law. She also lived in a nursing home in New York, and they had not been allowed to see her either since March.

"I am so afraid I will never see mom again," Tracy texted me.

Horses first raced here, in 1863, during the Civil War. The Saratoga Race Course survived two World Wars, the Depression, the Spanish Flu, and the Great Recession. This year, the races went on but with fans left to stand on the outside of the track looking in. Of course, even that view was limited, as Commissioner Dalton required the installation of privacy fencing around the entire facility to block such views.

So on July 16, we did the best we could and celebrated opening day like never before. Instead of watching the races inside the track, fans had more than two dozen restaurants that hosted viewing parties. "Lots of places in Saratoga to watch live horse racing, to gather with friends, to place a bet online, to enjoy some great food and drinks," I tweeted. "We're bringing the Grandstands into the community."

One of those viewing parties was at Racing City Brewing. That's where the Saratoga Crew planned to meet. We were joined there by the CEO of the New York Racing Association (NYRA) and several elected officials. The media was invited, and they were all there to do interviews about this unique summer in Saratoga.

"For racing-lovers like Dabreen Oliva, not being able to visit the Saratoga Race Course on Opening Day is a disappointment, but she and her staff are doing all they can to bring the same atmosphere to Racing City Brewing," Mark Mulholland said in his broadcast that night.

By 3:30 p.m., Ryan, Darryl, Deann, Sam, Shelby and me were the last ones from our group still there. Less than thirty minutes later, we watched as officials from the Public Safety department showed up. They had seen the media coverage and believed Racing City Brewing didn't have a permit to use the space where we were seated. As they approached the owner, one of them said they were there to shut the place down.

Ryan intervened directly with the city officials on site, and Darryl texted Robin Dalton. I called a friend in the public safety department as we all fought to stop this closure. The City didn't shut them down, but the next morning they ruled that this space could not be used again. This drastically reduced the seating capacity, a move that forced the brewery's owners to cancel hundreds of reservations and to close for good in the fall. The bad news didn't stop there for me on opening day.

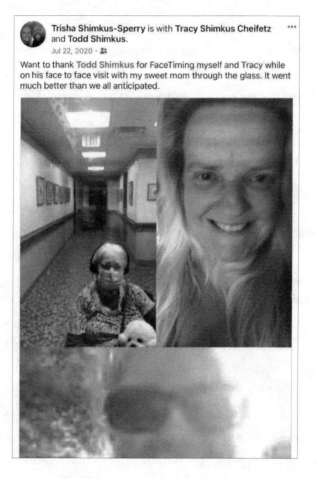

"I never ask for anything on Facebook and I never post my life here," said Trisha's husband, Rich Englund, late on July 16. "But my soul mate has now been admitted to the hospital with blood clots and I'm asking for a prayer to come her way. I love you Trisha."

That afternoon when Tyler returned home from school, he found his mom, Trisha, unconscious on the floor and called 911. An ambulance arrived and took her to the hospital. Because of COVID 19, neither her son, Tyler, nor Trisha's husband, Rich, could visit her, and just like our mom Trisha was scared, alone, and isolated from loved ones.

Trisha was diagnosed with an aortic thrombosis, and Tracy's husband Craig, who is a doctor, said this was serious and she was lucky she made it to the hospital. Just six weeks ago, Trisha and I had our worst fight ever; and we stopped talking. None of that mattered now.

"Not sure if you are able to get text messages but seriously please know I will drive there tonight if you need anything," I texted Trisha. "Cannot imagine how scary this must be. Love you, Todd." She replied: "My bloodwork is showing therapeutic levels so we are moving in the right direction. Love you."

Trisha was released from the hospital, and I promised to include her and Tracy virtually in my first window visit ever with our mom. Lisa decided to join me as we really had no idea how she'd react. My mom and I had not seen each other except on a screen in nearly 120 days.

Would she be confused? What should we say if she invited us to come inside? Was there any way to explain why we were on one side of the window and she was stuck on the other? Visiting my mom separated by a window didn't make sense to us, so how could we possibly explain this to someone with Alzheimer's.

We arrived ten minutes before our scheduled visit. I could see what looked like four areas set up for window visits. Each location had two chairs placed close to the window. There was a hand sanitizer station there too. Even though we were outdoors, the state required us to wear masks until we sat down like that made any sense, and we needed a cell phone to speak to her.

The nervousness I felt changed to excitement when I first saw her. She was in a wheelchair as a woman I didn't know brought her to the window. As she rolled closer, I waved both arms wildly to get her attention. She wore a mask so I could not see if she smiled until she came closer. Her escort put earphones on her head and stepped aside as I called in to the phone number posted on the outside wall.

My mom never said the words, "Hi Todd." Nor did she ask about Katie or Ben, so I didn't know whether or not she recognized me. She still carried her purse and Short Rib. I was glad to see he survived, but the purse made me think she might have thought she was going somewhere with me. With hairdressers locked out, her hair was longer than I had ever seen, and it was parted down the middle to keep it out of her eyes.

"Hi mom, it's Todd," I told her. "I brought Lisa with me. So great to see you. How are you?" She said she was good but didn't elaborate. Just as I did with every visit, I asked her my two go-to questions. How is your puppy? Did you go for a walk today?

What she said wasn't as important to me as it was to see her. Her long hair made her look older. With the layers of clothing she wore, I couldn't tell if she had lost any weight. As she arrived in a wheelchair, I had no idea if there were any changes in the way she walked. The fact that we could see each other made this better than a virtual visit, but not by much.

The window was a barrier that prevented us from making a meaningful connection. I'm sure the headphones felt funny to her, and while I was glad to see her, what I really wanted was to give her a hug, hold her hand, and let her know that we were really there with her. The good news was that she didn't appear confused by this situation, at least not at this visit.

As I promised, we used Lisa's phone to set up FaceTime so Tracy and Trisha could see and talk to her during this window visit. Twenty minutes later, her escort came over to let us know she had to bring my mom back to her room. "It was great to see you," I told my mom. "You look good. Don't work too hard today. We'll see you soon. I love you." Lisa, Tracy and Trisha all said goodbye too.

"It makes me so happy to just see and hear her," Tracy texted after. "Appreciate you sharing your time with her with us." On Facebook, Trisha posted: "Want to thank Todd for including myself and Tracy while on his visit with my sweet mom through the glass. It went much better than we all anticipated."

Saratoga's businesses were doing a little better too, at least the ones that were open as a smaller than usual steady stream of visitors did return. The second weekend of August was perhaps the busiest of the year, although that's not saying much. On Saturday, visitors and locals came out to viewing parties. They wanted to see Tiz the Law, a locally owned horse, win the Travers Stakes, at the Saratoga Race Course.

A friend, Bob Giordano, put Tiz the Law stickers on four stop signs outside his home that read: "STOP - Tiz the Law." The horse racing media around the world interviewed Bob about these signs and his love of horse racing. He was just having some fun to get some laughs. Commissioner Dalton didn't see the humor, and had the signs removed. The excitement for this local horse was real, but not universal.

On Wednesday, the City received a complaint from the New York State Liquor Authority (SLA) about a viewing party scheduled at a local hotel. They planned to host a viewing party for 50 of Tiz the Law's own-

ers and friends in their ballroom. They also planned to use space inside their restaurant to invite the general public to attend.

But, the SLA suggested that they viewed these two separate parties as one event and as configured that it would likely exceed public gathering limits. The hotel had no desire to be fined or shut down. So they opted to put everyone in the restaurant where tables were socially distanced from one another. Putting everyone in one room seemed less safe to me, but the state signed off on this change.

As a show of support for the hotel, Darryl, Shelby and I reserved a table and I invited Kevin Hedley, the Chair of the Chamber's Board of Directors, to join us. We watched NBC's live broadcast as Tiz the Law won the 151st Travers Stakes, and everyone jumped up and down to cheer as he crossed the finish line. After the party, Lisa and I raced out of Town. It was time for us to take a break.

It was not easy to vacation this summer. Governor Cuomo banned people from visiting New York from other states he deemed a risk. By early August, residents of more than 30 states were prohibited from traveling to New York. Virginia was on the banned list which made it impossible for Tracy to do a window visit with our mom.

As we looked for options to get away, Lisa and I decided to drive to York Beach, on the coast of Maine. This was one of the few states we could visit without having to quarantine ourselves for two weeks when we returned. Our plan was to sit on the beach, relax, and read a couple of books. One evening, we went for a walk along the Marginal

Way and stopped for dinner at an oceanfront restaurant with a huge outdoor patio.

The person sitting closest to us wore a Saratoga baseball cap, so I struck up a conversation with him. He normally visited Saratoga every year, but not with the track closed to fans. Just then, a woman at a nearby table asked, "Are you talking about Saratoga? We love it there. We would have been there this week if we could have gone to the track." Instead, we were all in York, Maine - gathered together safely outdoors helping their local economy recover.

On our final day, we met my cousin Jen for lunch at an outdoor patio overlooking the beach. Jen was the first close relative Lisa and I had seen since February. We hugged in the parking lot when we arrived and before we left for home, and the combination of taking a few days off to relax and being reunited with family was just what I needed to get re-energized.

Twenty minutes into our four hour drive home, my cell phone rang and when I saw it was my mom's nurse calling I picked it up right away. "Hi Todd, it's Dottie. Your mom fell this morning. It doesn't appear she was injured. We will monitor her situation and keep you posted."

My next window visit was not for four-days, and I now had to wait until then to see for myself how she looked. Meanwhile, the staff now checked on my mom every 15 minutes, not just because of this fall and her physical health. But also because her behavior towards the staff and other residents had become more aggressive and combative.

When we returned home, I waited anxiously for my next window visit and helped Lisa put the finishing touches on her latest masterpiece. "So here's what [Lisa] did this summer," I posted to Instagram. The post included what our home looked like before and after she painted it. She started this project as soon as her school's summer break began. Painting and being outdoors was therapeutic for her, especially after being forced to teach virtually.

Ben lived with us when she started this project. So he helped when he was not working at Target. No doubt our house needed to be painted. Where the sun shined brightest and longest, the red color had faded. Where the snow piled up against the house during winter, some of the shingles were worn.

Lisa and Ben were not the only ones who completed a home improvement project this year. People built new pools, kitchens, bathrooms, decks, additions, and fencing. Sales at Home Depot were up 23.4% from last year and Lowe's reported $27 billion in sales, compared with $21 billion a year ago. With stimulus funding in April from the Federal government, people had money to spend. We couldn't travel; so we fixed up our homes.

Our little house went from a faded red to a light shade of gray. On each side, Lisa found an area where she incorporated a wood feature. It was the flower boxes on one side, a window on the front, and a door on the back. She used white on the trim and there is a touch of dark green in several areas. The colors made the stone work on the house really pop.

"That's an amazing transformation," a neighbor told us when it was done. Seeing my post that this project was completed, her school's Principal commented: "And now she's all mine."

Lisa was making a move to protect herself from the virus. She thought she'd be safer if she taught first-graders, as they were the least likely to contract the virus. St Mary's planned to start the year in-school and capped class size at eighteen students - - the most possible while keeping desks six feet apart. Her first-graders completed kindergarten remotely, and it was likely they were less prepared than the typical first grader. This new challenge excited Lisa, as did the fact she would again be in her own classroom with her students in person.

On Monday, August 17, I went by myself for a window visit. I was anxious to see my mom after her fall. To my surprise, she looked fine, no different from my last visit. To wade through what might be real or imagined, I asked her a series of questions as I sought to figure out how she felt and if she was in any pain.

"Does your head hurt?," I asked her first. She said no. "How about your leg? Your arm? Your back?" No. No. No, she answered. Everything was fine on this day.

Trisha was not as lucky. The blood clots were the least of her worries. She had cancer, and it had spread from her colon to her ovary. Surgery was required followed by chemotherapy. "All I want to do is talk to my mom and have her say it will be okay," Trisha commented on Facebook. "But I can't. I'm broken. So very broken."

On this very day, there were just four Saratoga residents that tested positive and only two were hospitalized. All summer, we were spared in Saratoga from the worst of the virus. Only two employees at the Wesley had tested positive, and still not a single resident. Yet State protocols not only kept my mom isolated from us, they also kept Trisha away from her mom when she had cancer and needed her the most. Trisha said she was broken, and I would see at my next window visit that my mom was too.

Trisha Englund
Aug 20, 2020

Today is that moment. I got a call that potentially changed my life. I don't know what I don't know but the doctor seems to think it's urgent. So here I am on Facebook because all I want to do is talk to my mom and have her say it will all be ok. BUT I CANT! She is finally in a happy place. Alzheimer's tried to scare her before and I didn't want that for my lovely mother. She deserves to be so happy and loved. I miss talking with her so much. And not being able to tell her anything about me kills me a little more each day. I'm broken. So very broken. But also been the duck on water for so long that I have turned my tragedies into fake it till you make it. What ever happens to me I need everyone to know I truly am blessed to have good friends loving family, soulmate- Rich Englund and my heart - Tyler all in my life right now. I'm scared but it is still

I wasn't broken, but I was being criticized. After the County voted to fund our ad campaign, an official who voted against this request posted a meme on Twitter critical of my efforts. When I saw the meme, I contacted county leaders and within hours this official deleted his entire Twitter account.

Commissioner Dalton emailed the Chamber's Board of Directors and suggested some of my comments to her during the debate on outdoor patios was "offensive, disrespectful, and unprofessional." Kevin Hedley thanked her for her vote to expand the outdoor patios and indicated that I had the Board's continued support.

None of this bothered me, as I understood this is what happens when you take a stand to lead a community in a crisis. But in late-August, I was attacked in a manner that shocked me both in terms of what was said and who said it.

In the first days of the pandemic, Shelby created a shared Zoom account that all of our organizations could use as well as the Saratoga Economic Development Corporation (SEDC). Dennis Brobston, the President of SEDC, was at our March 13th meeting where we agreed to work together. But soon after that meeting, he went AWOL and stopped communicating with us, but SEDC continued to use this Zoom account.

Even a novice user of Zoom quickly learned that you had the option of recording or not recording online Zoom meetings. But for whatever reason in early August, the four employees of SEDC recorded a video of one of their staff meeting on Zoom. In this video, Tori Riley - - who I hired to work with me at the Adirondack Chamber a dozen years before - - called Shelby and me "pigs."

The first time I watched this video I was home, and Lisa was in the living room where she could hear every word. "Is that Tori Riley saying those things about you," Lisa asked. I said yes. "Didn't you hire her to work with you at the Adirondack Chamber? Didn't you recommend her for that SEDC job?" I told Lisa she was correct on both accounts.

In the video, Dennis made fun of me for being short, and mimicked me in an unflattering way. What he said and did was childish and unprofessional, but what Tori said was despicable and hurtful. The only smart comment in the hour-long meeting was from a third employee who suggested the video be deleted, which they never did.

"Somebody discarded inappropriate things in the parking lot [referring to a condom]. It was all I could do not to put gloves on and leave it on Todd's car," Tori said on the video. "Shelby and Todd are like pigs in a trough. They will use and abuse and do whatever they can. It's never to your benefit," she added as Dennis just laughed.

I was not the only community leader they denigrated with vulgar language. They attacked anyone that had ever supported merging SEDC with the Prosperity Partnership. Two days later, I gave the chairman of the SEDC Board a copy of the video, and he suspended Dennis and Tori immediately. A full SEDC board meeting was scheduled and an attorney secured to discuss what the organization should and could do.

In my role as Chamber President, I was a voting member of SEDC's Board, so I was in the room in late-August when we all watched the video. "Todd, I want to apologize to you for what was said and for you having to sit here and watch that with us. I'm sure that could not have been easy," one of the Board members said. The Board then voted unanimously to terminate Tori's employment immediately and to ask Dennis to resign within six months. I felt vindicated and expected these actions would put an end to this situation, but it did not.

SEPTEMBER 2020

ON SEPTEMBER 1, I was in for another disturbing surprise. Lisa and I went for our now once-a-week 20 minute window visit with my mom. When we arrived, she was already at the window, and I could tell she was not in good shape. We took our masks off and sat down. I moved my chair as close to the window as possible, as if my being closer to the window made any difference.

My mom's eyes were closed, and her mask was under her chin. Her head tilted down as she sobbed. For the first time, she had a belt around her waist, one that I knew was used to help lift residents up when they could not stand on their own. She loosely held her dog, and it looked like he might fall to the ground at any time. I knocked on the window. Normally, she smiled back at me, but not today.

Reluctantly, she allowed her escort to put on the headphones so I could speak to her. "Hi mom, it's Todd and Lisa. What's wrong? Do you feel okay?" I asked her. At first, it was hard to understand what she said in response. Her voice was so soft, no louder than a whisper. She rambled words we couldn't understand. Then there was a moment of pure clarity.

"I just want to go home," she said. "I want to go home. Where is my car? They won't tell me where my car is. I just want to go home. Why doesn't anyone visit me? No one cares. No one is helping me."

My mom was in tears, and Lisa started to cry too. We were not prepared for this. There was no way for us to know what caused this depression. Was it the fall? The loneliness and isolation? Lack of sleep? Did she really think no one cared? I looked right at her, as my eyes welled up with tears and I tried to think of something to say.

"Mom, we are right here," I told her. "We love you. I wish I could get in there to give you a hug right now. That would be nice, right?" She

nodded slightly. "I'd be willing to break this glass to give you a hug, but I don't think anyone would like that."

This was the first time since the lockdown began where it was absolutely clear that she needed to be with us. She was inside, and we were out and this meant none of us could give her a hug, hold her hand, or rub her shoulders so she could physically feel that we were there to support her. Mere words through a headset could not improve her disposition, so I improvised as best I could.

I held my right hand out, and put my hand on the outside of the window. "Mom, please put your hand on the window. Right here," I said as I tapped my fingers on the window. She was still looking down at her lap. "Mom, please put your hand on the window where mine is."

Her right hand slowly inched up until she touched the inside of the glass. With her hand on the window, I said, "See mom, it's like we're holding hands right now. Everything will be okay. I love you. I am going to make some calls to see if we can do something to help you. Would you like me to do that? Is that okay with you? I will make some calls. I promise."

Her hand went back to her lap. She mumbled something else that we couldn't understand. She never looked up and did not smile once. Her escort came over and asked my mom if she wanted to go back, and my mom nodded yes. "I love you mom. We both love you. I will see you soon," I said as this person removed the headset.

I told Tracy and Trisha to expect my call and that I would Face-Time with them during this visit, but I didn't. When the visit ended, I called them right away to share what happened. Now everyone was upset.

"Today, I am asking for all your prayers," Trisha posted. "Not for me, even though I can use them with all that is happening. But for my mother. This disease sucks and I don't want to ever see her in pain or sadness. I don't pray in a church, but I hope and pray daily for someone to come and bless my mom."

When my mom said, "I want to go home," I think she told us how much she missed us. If she had been allowed to get her car, the most likely destination she would have driven to was one of our homes. Later that night, she became weepy and when asked what was wrong she told the nurse she was "worried about the babies." As she tried and failed to explain herself further, she sobbed even harder.

Now I had proof that the nursing home visitation policies in New York needed to be changed. They completely neglected the mental health needs of residents, like my mom, as they faced this prolonged isolation from loved ones. Maybe this kept them safe from the virus, but that didn't mean they didn't suffer. I know my mom did, and this was so unfair.

Lisa Davis Shimkus
Aug 31, 2020

Really feeling like a first grade teacher now!

Nursing homes were still locked down, but the Governor allowed schools to re-open after Labor Day. As Lisa switched to first grade, she knew her 18 students were likely less prepared than any first-graders in recent memory. Everything about school and being with other people would be new to them.

The faculty and students were required to wear masks and to practice social distancing. Each class was organized like a self-contained pod with separate lunches and recesses. Everyone had their temperature taken every morning. If you had so much as a runny nose or cough, you were told to stay home and to test negative before you could return.

The school installed clear plastic barriers on the desks, teachers kept their windows open as much as possible. The Principal still did his daily announcements and morning prayer virtually, as each class watched on their smart boards. The students were required to use hand sanitizer every time they went in or out of the classroom. It was a totally new routine for everyone.

Often with much higher class sizes, most public schools adopted a hybrid model. Their students spent two or three days at school per week, and the balance at home online. This was required to ensure social distancing in classrooms, cafeterias, gyms and on buses. This hybrid model was not ideal for working parents, nor as we would later learn with declining test results it also did not provide the best educational opportunities.

St Mary's benefitted from the pandemic, in a way. Many parents realized the benefits of in-person learning for their children and themselves, and that's why this private school filled up all of their classrooms to capacity. People were willing to pay tuition so that their children could be in-school full-time and they could work.

"I am so excited to get back into the classroom," Lisa posted as she wore a crayola crayon inspired mask. "Great principal, wonderful faculty. Love this little school." Lisa bonded instantly with these students, and she was happy with her choice to move to first grade. But she was not happy with me that night.

Just as Lisa's first day of school came to an end, the Saratoga Crew gathered at a local bar and we ordered our first of many drinks. Darryl shared preliminary estimates of summer hotel occupancy, and it looked like a 75 percent decline from the prior year. This was devastating to Darryl and Ryan, whose organizations relied on occupancy taxes to fund their operations.

Shelby and I were upset as Dennis somehow convinced a majority of the SEDC Board to reinstate him and Tori. They now publicly accused Shelby of illegally accessing and sharing the video in which they attacked us. This left me with no choice but to resign from this Board along with three other members.

Of course, we still didn't know what caused my mom's meltdown. She needed us to be with her, and I knew there were safe options to do so. With each day we were kept apart, I became more and more furious at the Governor, and frustrated that there was nothing I could do to help my mom.

Lisa was excited to share some of her fun first-day-of-school stories with me, but by the time I got home I was too drunk to listen. As we both knew, I had been drinking too much all summer. Maybe this was the result of the stress of my job, the inability to help my mom, the trauma of the disruption to our lives caused by the pandemic, or that I felt safe to let loose and have fun when I was drinking with the Crew.

Numerous studies showed I was not alone and that alcohol consumption increased in all demographics during the pandemic. The Journal of American Medicine reported that alcohol related deaths increased 25 percent in 2020 versus 2019. Local wine and liquor stores, deemed essential and allowed to stay open, reported record breaking revenue in 2020.

The next morning, my plan was to take more time off to relax and to run more often. My gym was finally allowed to reopen, and I signed up for at least one class per week. This was when I decided to try to write this book. The goal was to spend more time working out, running, reading, and writing instead of working and drinking.

Just a couple days later, I fell for one of the Governor's tricks. He finally announced a relaxation of nursing home visitation policies. In particular, the waiting period for a facility-wide quarantine after an employee tested positive was finally reduced to the federal 14-day standard. So as long as no additional Wesley employees tested positive, I would be allowed to visit my mom outdoors in early October.

It had been 180 days since I last hugged her, and I believed our being together would help her. So when a local reporter called me for a comment, I said: "I just want to see my mom. You could have told me to do cartwheels and douse myself in hand sanitizer and I would have done it. So whatever I've got to do so she knows I'm there. I'm going to do it."

I signed up to visit her on October 5. The visit would be outside under one of the tents the Wesley put up months ago. In the meantime, I did another window visit on September 23, and my mom looked better. Because he is a doctor, we asked Craig to speak with mom's nurse about modifications to her medications, and this helped a little.

On this day, as my mom and I sat across from each other separated by a window, Trisha was in surgery. Her doctors removed as much of the cancer as possible and inserted a port to assist with chemotherapy treatments. She too was doing whatever was required to live and to be reunited someday with our mom.

I didn't share Trisha's situation with anyone. She texted me from the hospital and vowed to fight to see Tyler graduate, so I went about my work. Today, I toured a local photographer's new studio. Besides the tour, he offered to shoot a new professional headshot for me.

I now wore a "Stronger Together Saratoga County" mask everywhere, every day. I tried to set a good example. I figured health care workers had to do it as did the heroes at the Wesley. Lisa and her first grade students were masked up, and it was a small sacrifice for me to make to follow their lead.

But I did not wear a suit or tie anymore. There was no reason to dress up when we worked from home. Everyone on Zoom

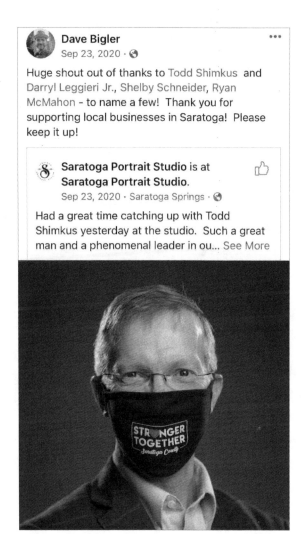

dressed casually, and some were perhaps too casual. My work clothes now consisted of khaki pants and either a button down shirt or Chamber logo golf shirt. I might occasionally add a jacket.

So I told the photographer I wanted a "pandemic headshot." This became my social media profile picture. When the media asked me for a photo, this is what I gave them. I posed wearing a mask, a button down shirt, a jacket and no tie. Not everyone thought masks worked, this included the President of the United States who relied more on testing to protect himself.

OCTOBER 2020

ON OCTOBER 2, 2020, President Trump tested positive for COVID 19. He was now among the more than seven million Americans who had tested positive for the virus so far in 2020. Soon the President was hospitalized, his departure from the White House live-streamed on all networks. I remember thinking that if he could get it, so could anyone else. Yet I wasn't sure he took all of the precautions recommended by health experts either.

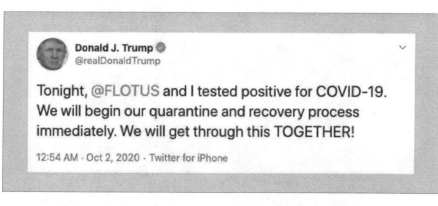

Three days later, the President tweeted: "I will be leaving the great Walter Reed Medical Center. Feeling really good! We have developed some really great drugs and knowledge. I feel better than I did 20 years ago."

Like our Governor, the President was now a conquering hero to his followers. He proved that the virus could be beaten. His followers continued to champion respect for an individual's right to wear a mask or not. As President Trump said, they believed that no one should let the virus dominate your life.

Meanwhile, Governor Cuomo continued to do the opposite. He believed the government had a responsibility to protect us, since

COVID-19 was a public health emergency. So in New York, gatherings were still limited and social distancing was still required. We had a mask mandate. Most businesses—even those who were open — could do so only if they abided by state imposed capacity limitations.

In terms of fighting the virus, this clear difference of opinion and the confidence each side demonstrated that they were right made it hard to know what worked and what didn't. For instance, Saratoga Hospital's COVID-19 team told local restaurant owners and school superintendents that universal masking worked at the hospital. As soon as they implemented that one protocol, they had no more spread of the virus in their facility. That's exactly why I never hesitated to wear a mask and advised others to do the same.

But in other states, like Texas and Florida, there was never a mask mandate. Many sectors of their economies were allowed to reopen fully without restrictions, and they never seemed to suffer more hospitalizations or deaths than we did in New York. The virus surged and receded at different times in these states just as it did here, and was no more or less deadly.

In Saratoga, just 17 people had died from the virus in a population of 230,000 people. The reopening committee was told that all of them had underlying health conditions. Did the deaths stop locally because of the lockdown or the mask mandate? Was it climate related? Did the virus recede when it was warm and most people gathered outside? Medical experts suggested all sorts of theories as did our politicians, but I don't believe we ever really knew what worked and what didn't.

Clearly, seniors and those with comorbidities so far were at far greater risk than the general population. But did keeping them safe require limits on everyone's freedom? Or would it be safer to urge older people to take responsibility for protecting themselves? These questions and the conflict on how best to fight this virus raged on as the virus surged again, again, and again.

I thought it had been safe enough to visit my mom outside since June. But I didn't get to actually visit with her until October 5. This "tent visit," as the Wesley called it, was memorable for all the wrong reasons.

"Just finished a so-called in-person visit with mom," I texted Tracy and Trisha. "Window visits are better. They took a photo of us outside the tent. We had to stay six feet apart. No hugs."

To see my mom, the rules required me to have a negative COVID-19 test within 7 days of my visit. This was a totally useless protocol, as I did not need to quarantine after I tested until I saw my mom. This meant there was plenty of opportunity for me to catch the virus after the test without ever knowing it, but I took the test anyway.

I was not allowed to arrive on the Wesley property until 15 minutes before the visit. With window visits, I could take my mask off when I sat down so my mom could see my face. But today I had to wear a mask at all times as did she. There was no requirement on the type of mask so I wore my Stronger Together cloth mask to cover my nose and mouth. Months later, the CDC would advise that cloth masks really didn't work.

Outside of the tent, I walked up to a registration table and told the woman stationed there my name and who I was scheduled to visit. She asked me for my license and a copy of my negative test result. She was required to make sure the name on the test and the license matched. She took my temperature and asked me to use hand sanitizer.

Then I affirmed in writing that I tested negative, and had not traveled to any banned state, or been in contact with anyone with COVID-19. They also asked if I had lost my sense of taste or smell. This question might have seemed odd, but one of the most common symptoms of those who had the virus was a loss of these senses. I had never lost either.

Days earlier, the Wesley's public relations team asked if they could take a photo of my mom and me during this visit. Our photo would accompany a press release that announced they were now allowed to host in-person visits. I said yes and was escorted to an area just outside the tent. My mom was there already, and I saw her sitting in a wheelchair.

She had a white and purple blanket draped over her. She wore a mask and somebody else's sunglasses. I was surprised she did not have her dog, purse or purple jacket.

Just a few days earlier, I saw a post on Facebook from a friend from high school who had been able to visit her mom in a nursing home in Massachusetts. "Tonight was the first time I could actually feel my mom's touch since March," she said. "Despite the hand sanitizer and masks, it was still miraculous. Don't EVER take the power of touch for granted."

Here in New York, no touching or hugs were allowed. Even outside, we had to stay six feet apart, a small distance in reality but one that seemed gigantic on this day. My mom was right there, but I could not reach out to make contact.

I waved and said: "Hi mom, it's Todd. It's so good to see you." She just smiled back. This must have been so confusing. Why was she outside? Why didn't I give her a hug? This, of course, assumed she even knew who I was with my face hidden behind the mask.

After the photo, I was led into the tent and told to sit in a chair behind a clear plastic barrier. My mom was wheeled into position facing me on the other side of the barrier. To keep the tent warm, there was a portable heater with a blower and it made noise. My escort moved to where she could watch us, as if a guard needed to monitor our every move.

Seeing her wrapped in the blanket, I asked my mom if she was warm enough, but I couldn't make out what she said in response. She spoke again but I still couldn't hear her. I sat up, leaned toward her and asked her about her dog. I could see her mask move and knew she said something but I still didn't hear a word she said. I turned to the escort and told her I couldn't hear my mom.

The escort came over with a chair and sat down with my mom. Initially, this ticked me off — I should have been the one who sat right next to her. But I reminded myself that she was just trying to help and she didn't make the rules. I smiled as I thought to myself that there's no way this will work.

By this time, Alzheimer's was slowly taking away my mom's ability to communicate with us. She no longer spoke in full sentences, nor did she always use real words. We adapted to this in our virtual and window visits by making sure to pick out one sentence or one word we recognized to extend our conversations with her. To do this, I needed to hear every word she said to find one to use, and there was no chance the escort knew how to do this.

But this visit was not supposed to be about hearing her — we could already do that virtually or through a window. It should have been about me being with her and us making a real connection again. There was no chance a quick hug outdoors with a mask on in a community where the spread of the virus was still low would be harmful. Yet it might have helped her immensely even if the contact lasted just a few seconds.

I had no choice and decided to play along. "How are you feeling?" I asked her. The escort listened carefully, and then just looked at me as she did not know what mom said or what to say to me. At that point, we both very clearly heard my mom say one word: bathroom. There were no restrooms in the tent, nor CNA's available to help her. So I decided to end the visit.

"I think she needs to go to the bathroom," I said. "Can you take her please? I'll just say goodbye now." I looked directly at my mom and told her that I loved her and would see her soon. The escort whisked her out of the tent. I slowly walked to my car, angry, disappointed, sad. This was not fair, inhumane really. That night, my mom was reported by the staff to present with separation anxiety, as all she remembered was that I left her there again.

"Amy had been accustomed to frequent visits from son prior to initiation of visitation restrictions, and has had some difficulty adapting to the changes," one staff member wrote in a report. "This is likely related to dementia and inability to understand rationale as well as having been accustomed to being able to visit regularly."

I had not seen my mom in over 200 days. Sitting next to me was just as safe as sitting next to the escort, maybe safer. I wore a mask whenever I was in public. I had not yet been in contact with anyone who'd tested positive for the virus. At this point, I was never quarantined, nor did I ever feel sick or catch a cold in 2020. None of this mattered. Governor Cuomo said the escort could sit next to my mom, and I could not.

Except for virtual visits, Tracy had not seen our mom in person in 9 months. So when, on October 8th without any explanation, Virginia was removed from Cuomo's travel ban list, Tracy asked if I could schedule her for a window visit. Four days later, she drove eight hours to get here. It was Columbus Day, so Lisa had the day off.

Rather than staying with us, Tracy rented a room at a local hotel just to be safe. When the three of us went out to dinner, we picked a restaurant where we could sit outdoors that also had portable heaters. The portable heater near us stopped working, so Tracy went to her car and grabbed a bunch of blankets for us to use to stay warm. What we did to be together safely was just so weird still.

The next morning, she and I went to see our mom. "Last week, Virginia was removed from the NY travel ban," Tracy posted on Facebook. "Not sure how long it would last, I drove up to Saratoga to have a 15 minute window visit with my mom before driving back. THANKFULLY had a nice visit (albeit through a window). Not sure she knew who I was, but I had the boys record videos. I think watching her reaction to those it was clear she knows she loves us!"

Just like Tracy and me, the one thing Trisha wanted more than anything was to be able to spend time with our mom. Unfortunately, she was unable to come to Saratoga this fall as her cancer and surgery placed her in a compromised position. But Tracy had an idea to connect the two of them.

Tracy still had our mom's favorite blanket and some of her perfume. Neither of these items went with our mom to the Wesley, but now Tracy created a care package with them and sent it to Trisha. "I am hugging the blanket as if to finally give my mom the hug I have needed to give her since COVID began," Trisha said in a post. I am crying because it smells like her."

My mom had her stuffed animal Ribbie, and now Trisha had mom's blanket. Each of these objects comforted them as they faced their trauma. Trisha felt like my mom gave her a hug, and my mom took Ribbie for a walk every day. There's no chance I'd ever think to give either of these gifts to my mom or Trisha. But, I'm so glad Trisha and Tracy did.

As Tracy drove home, Virginia was put back on New York's travel ban list. Later that week, a Wesley employee tested positive and window visits were canceled. We hoped this situation would be temporary, but a second wave was building. This one would be far more deadly than the first, including inside the Wesley.

The summer surge of visitors never materialized. So as Fall began, it was no secret to anyone who spoke with local business owners: they were still in survival mode. With no end in sight to the pandemic and business restrictions, we needed to do something to help them.

The Saratoga Crew talked about replacing our traditional Victorian Stroll with a Christmas Tree display downtown to attract shoppers. Darryl spoke to city leaders about the potential to build an ice skating rink in Congress Park. The Chamber staff discussed Black Friday and Small Business Saturday, but we worried because these promotions were a month away, and our local businesses needed more than a one or two-day boost.

That's when we created a first-ever, "Save Our Locals" campaign. Our goal was to raise $10,000 to do boosted posts that featured local products and services from mid-October to the New Year. Without tourists, we needed local people to shop for products and services locally as often as they could.

Like our Stronger Together campaign, the "Save Our Locals" logo and posters featured a heart with rainbow colors. As we launched this promotion, donations poured in and we collected $50,000. A local bank let us use a billboard they owned and a local engraving company etched the "Save Our Locals" logo on pumpkins that were donated by a local farm. Everywhere you looked in Saratoga and online, there were reminders to save our locals.

On October 20, Katie and I did our part to Save Our Locals. I sent her an electronic gift card so she could purchase some designer donuts and a coffee. She had done nearly the exact same thing for me. "Ooooh, if you're home, the Death Wish Coffee package that came for me is actually for you," she responded.

With travel restrictions in place, this was the best we could do on a day that we typically celebrated secretly together. It was on this day, in 1993, that we officially became father and daughter. We call it, "Adoption Day."

Her biological father was never interested in being a dad. He and Lisa were in college when Katie was born. The two of them split up soon after Lisa became pregnant, and she moved back home to live with her mom, Terry.

When I got my first real job after college, Terry was a co-worker. That night, she mentioned to Lisa that the organization hired a new guy. "Is he cute?" Lisa asked. Terry responded, "He looks like he's twelve."

I first met Lisa when she was pregnant and came to the office to visit Terry. After Katie was born, she visited more often and we started to talk. I invited Terry, Lisa and Katie to a New Year's Day breakfast I hosted for friends and family. The next July, I was invited to Katie's first birthday party. Lisa and I married in late 1992. Katie was two and a flower girl at our wedding.

Adoption Day was the day Lisa, Katie, Terry and I went to meet with a Family Court Judge to get the petition signed. She had always called me Daddy-Todd or just Daddy. But on this day when the judge asked Katie who I was, Katie replied, "Todd." Lisa, Terry and I just laughed.

After we left court, our families gathered to celebrate the first Adoption Day. From that point forward, it became a day for Katie and me to celebrate with cake or donuts. We've both posted photos of our birthdays, and we've done the same with holiday photos. But neither of us has ever posted about Adoption Day. That's because we're just Katie and dad.

In 2020, Halloween was different too as many people didn't feel safe handing out candy to children, and parents didn't feel safe taking their children to other people's homes.

So there could be some trick-or-treating, a local catering company came up with a safer alternative called "Spooktacular 2020." The Chamber set up a website that allowed people to buy a ticket for a specific time to drive their car through SPAC's grounds. The company set up tables at certain intervals and volunteers dressed up in costumes. The volunteers used devices to grab and drop candy through open car windows into children's bags, buckets or laps while everyone stayed safely in their cars.

Darryl and I volunteered to give out candy. Lucky for him, I had two horse costumes. Thankfully, Sam showed up to help us get into them, as it was not easy to do on our own. She took photos and videos of this process that were quickly circulated on social media. Ryan's wife wrote on Facebook: "Note that the woman (Sam) in the middle has chosen to hide her identity rather than having to explain her association with these two."

In two nights, more than 1,000 cars packed with children safely drove through Spooktacular. Not everyone spent Halloween as safely as we did. Gatherings of family and friends for Halloween became super-spreader events as a frightening second wave approached.

THE 2020 HOLIDAY SEASON

FOR THE FIRST TIME, on November 9, a Wesley resident tested positive. The staff had heroically kept COVID-19 out of the facility for seven months. We thought the separation from loved ones was bad, but now my mom was unable to leave her room. "Mom is now truly in jail," Tracy said after reading the notice from the Wesley.

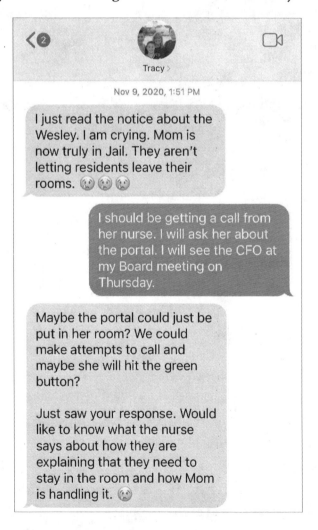

While residents were quarantined as much as possible in their rooms, the Wesley employees now wore head-to-toe personal protection equipment, including: masks, gowns, gloves, and goggles. For some residents, they already had a hard time recognizing one another and the staff. Now their daily routines were changed and the staff would be unrecognizable.

When I was allowed to visit before the shutdown, I often watched as employees held a resident's hand to calm them down or to direct them on where to go. They gave residents hugs or rubbed their backs when they looked lost, confused, upset or cried. This was in addition to the help the staff provided so each resident could get dressed, bathed, fed, medicated, put to bed and to the bathroom.

Close physical interaction of any kind between the residents and staff was dangerous, life threatening really as we soon learned. This meant group activities were curtailed. No more art, music, or the opportunity to watch old movies together. Communal dining was limited, as it was safer for residents to eat in their own room.

One day earlier, the Saratoga Crew learned that Sam's dad passed away unexpectedly. This news was so devastating that she didn't share it publicly for nearly a year. Like my mom, her dad had Alzheimer's.

"I was fortunate that my dad still knew me when he passed," she shared on Facebook on Father's Day in 2021. "While it was difficult for my mom, I found peace in that nearly every night he asked my mom when I was coming home or visiting and if my dog, Leo, needed to be let inside. He loved Leo."

Like my mom, Sam's dad worried every day about his child and her dog. The similarities between our situations was striking. But now her dad was at peace, his battle with this miserable disease over with his loving wife by his side until the end.

I felt terrible for Sam. Losing a parent sucks no matter when or how. As I tried to comfort her, I was left to wonder which was the lesser of two evils. Was Sam's dad in a better place now than my mom? Thousands had already died in New York's nursing homes since the start of the pandemic. Were they actually the lucky ones?

What happened to my mom and the nursing home residents who survived since March across New York was not fair. No one should have to face Alzheimer's or the end of their lives alone, isolated from the ones they love. Not even during a pandemic. My mom was not at peace, she was "in jail," alive and all alone.

My mom did not do well confined to her room. There, she had a roommate, a television, lots of pictures and her dog, but little else to keep her busy or comforted. Soon she would take her frustration out on others more frequently and more violently.

The second wave spread quickly, millions across the US and the world would get sick. Rather than another full shutdown, the Governor imposed a broad array of new limits to restrict people from gathering in specific places.

For instance, the Governor announced that any establishment with a state liquor license, including bars and restaurants, had to close at 10:00 p.m. These businesses also could not serve alcohol to customers unless they purchased food. This curfew was extended to gyms.

Here we go again, I thought as I wondered why 10 p.m? This random time made even less sense for a gym. After I spoke with a gym owner, I tweeted what he told me: "You know who goes to the gym after 10:00 p.m? The people who want to avoid crowds when they workout."

The Governor then attempted to extend his control directly into people's homes. "We know indoor gatherings and parties are a major source of COVID spread," he told us. "To slow the spread, New York State will limit indoor gatherings at private residences to 10 people." With the holidays coming, this rule was met with outrage.

"In response to numerous inquiries about whether the Sheriff's Office intends to enforce Governor Cuomo's Executive Order limiting the number of guests at Thanksgiving gatherings, the Saratoga County Sheriff's Office will not do so," said a press release. "The Sheriff's

Office encourages the public to use common sense and to follow best practices during these uncertain times. If you are sick, you should not be out in public. As always, citizens are reminded to wear masks and to wash hands frequently."

Saratoga County Sheriff's Office
Nov 16, 2020 ·

Sheriff Zurlo's statement on Thanksgiving Executive Order.

SARATOGA COUNTY SHERIFF'S OFFICE
Sheriff@SaratogaCountyNY.gov

MICHAEL H. ZURLO
SHERIFF

Richard L. Castle
Undersheriff

Glenn D. Sheehy
Chief Deputy

PRESS RELEASE

For Release: Immediately
Instagram: Saratogasheriff
Snapchat: Saratoga County Sheriff's Office
YouTube: Saratoga County Sheriff's Office

INTERNET DISTRIBUTION AUTHORIZED
Facebook: SaratogaCountySheriff
Twitter: @Saratogasheriff
Website: www.saratogacountysheriff.org

November 16, 2020

In response to numerous inquiries about whether the Sheriff's Office intends to enforce Governor Cuomo's Executive Order limiting the number of guests at Thanksgiving gatherings to 10 people or less, the Saratoga County Sheriff's Office will not do so.

Sheriff Michael H. Zurlo commented, "We've seen an increase in a variety of call types and have to prioritize. I can't see how devoting our resources to counting cars in our citizens' driveways or investigating how much turkey and dressing they've purchased is for the public good."

The Sheriff's Office considers its citizens' private residences sacrosanct and as always will respect this. It is the agency's position that who and how many people a citizen decides to host for Thanksgiving dinner is outside the realm of governmental oversight.

The Sheriff's Office encourages the public to use common sense and follow best practices during these uncertain times. If you are sick, COVID positive, or otherwise at an increased risk, you should not be out in public regardless of the holiday. As always, citizens are reminded to wear masks in public and to wash their hands frequently.

"I encourage everybody to act responsibly," Sheriff Zurlo stated. "On behalf of the men and women of the Saratoga County Sheriff's Office, I wish you the happiest of Thanksgivings and a Merry Christmas."

###

Besides being impossible to enforce, the limit of ten people in a home was arbitrary. For example, my home is just 1,200 square feet. To be able to safely spend Thanksgiving together with Katie and Ben, Lisa and I were smart and got creative. By comparison, Tracy's home is three stories with a screened in deck and a large yard. She could have hosted dozens of people and kept them socially distant and safe.

Since the pandemic began, I allowed myself to quietly question some rules and protocols imposed supposedly for our safety. When I could, I enjoyed a little subtle defiance at several points along the way. For instance in the early days, just going to my office was questionable, but I often walked to work while I kept the shades drawn tight and of course the Saratoga Crew met in person every week.

After we entered phase 3 of the reopening, the Chamber began to host in-person ribbon cuttings again, and we did 48 before the end of the year. In terms of attendance, the largest of these was on November 10 to celebrate the opening of the City Center's new parking garage. A day later, a local television reporter reached out and told me several viewers called to suggest they investigate to see if we broke any COVID-19 protocols at this event.

"Can't we celebrate anything," Samantha texted after I shared this. "Good thing I wasn't there. I perhaps would have been the person that put you over 50 people. Haha!"

I looked at all of the photos and counted 45 people at most. The event was outdoors and we asked everyone to wear a mask. We stayed socially distant except for the one minute it took for the ribbon cutting photo. At the end of the interview, I reminded the reporter that on that very day there were just eleven active cases in the city.

With Thanksgiving coming, I now took it as a personal challenge to find a way to celebrate Thanksgiving together at our home with Lisa, Katie, Ben and me. All four of us were surviving, not thriving, so I did not think it was a good idea for us to be alone.

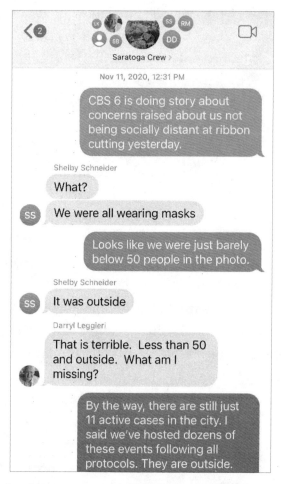

For Ben, the theaters were still closed, so he was working at Target in Brooklyn. As he worked there, he experienced the plight of many essential front-line service workers; low pay, long hours, and being forced to deal with people who cared more about their own personal liberty than the health of those around them. Many customers refused to wear a mask, and some were belligerent when asked to do so.

On November 13, Katie was told that her job at the bookstore would be eliminated at the end of the year. If she didn't find work, how could she afford to stay in Boston? As she looked for a new job, she tried to figure out how to apply for unemployment, and all of this uncertainty and change made her anxious.

Just days before Thanksgiving, I shared my plan with everyone. I reserved Katie and Ben separate rooms at a hotel a half mile from our house. Ben rented a car, and agreed to drive to Boston to pick up Katie. They could wear masks and drive together to Saratoga with the windows open. This seemed safer than taking a train or bus.

At the Chamber, I told everyone to work from home for the two weeks around Thanksgiving. I didn't want to have to track who went where or who stayed with them over the Holidays. Nor did I want them to ask me about Ben and Katie. I urged everyone to have fun, safely.

I pre-ordered Thanksgiving dinners to-go and separate take-out dinners from another local restaurant we all loved. These meals were all individually packaged and could be reheated whenever we were hungry. Each meal had so much food that we all had left-overs.

The four of us spent most of our time together on our front porch. Lisa and I sat on the swing. Six feet away, Katie sat in a swivel chair. Six feet from her, Ben sat in another one. I purchased two space heaters, and one was aimed at Lisa and my feet while the other pointed towards Katie and Ben. Each of us had a winter hat, jacket, gloves, as well as blankets.

Our windows were kept open just a little, this allowed the air to circulate. We each went into the house by ourselves, masked, to get our own food, drink, or to use the bathroom. Masks stayed on except when we ate or drank. We talked about the election, the pandemic, the future of theater and bookstores, sports, news, and how silly we looked to anyone who walked by our house.

None of us contracted the virus after this gathering. Neither did anyone on the Chamber's staff or in the Saratoga Crew. We were safe not because of some government edict, but because we creatively figured out how to travel and gather safely. Of course, we were not able to see my mom, not even virtually. That's because the latest test results weren't back before the Holiday. All we knew was that Tracy spoke to her the day before, and our mom had no idea Thanksgiving was this week.

Not everyone got through Thanksgiving unscathed. At Lisa's school, the principal was forced to quarantine along with his sister, a Spanish teacher. Both attended the same family gathering, and a few days later their father tested positive. The principal and Spanish teacher had moved from classroom to classroom the week before the Holiday weekend. Now if either of them tested positive, it was likely the school would be closed.

The Chamber's Board of Directors was scheduled to meet in-person at the City Center, on December 10. Two days before this meeting, a member of the Board posted that her husband had been in the hospital's intensive care unit with the virus, and now she had a head cold. She stayed home and missed the meeting.

By this time, most local organizations stopped hosting in-person meetings, but not the Chamber. To be safe, these meetings were held at the City Center. The capacity of the room where we met was 500, and we capped our meeting at 25 people.

I'M NOT READY FOR THIS...

Just as we did for the Saratoga Crew, each attendee had their own six-foot table and one chair. These tables stretched so far in the room that we needed microphones to hear what people said from the other side of the room. Attendees wore masks and were not allowed to gather before or after the meeting. No one ever contracted the virus at these meetings.

The first days of December saw thousands of Americans perish. More than 2,400 on December 1; 2,700 the next day; and 2,861, the day after that. CBS News shared a chart, created by "The Political Wire," which compared these days with some of our nation's other deadliest days.

On December 14, the Associated Press tweeted: "The U.S. death toll from the coronavirus topped 300,000 today. The number of dead is equivalent to repeating a tragedy on the scale of Hurricane Katrina every day for 5 ½ months." Other posts compared our COVID death toll with the 116,000 Americans killed in World War I; or the 405,000 who died in World War II; or the 675,000 who perished in the Great Pandemic of 1917.

Ironically, this was the very day that Americans started to roll up their sleeves. Launched in May, President Trump's "Warp Speed" project to save the world from the virus had come to fruition, and a vaccine was approved by the FDA for emergency use. The race was now on to manufacture hundreds of millions of doses and to set up a nationwide mass vaccination campaign.

The New York Times declared: "When future historians close the books on 2020, a grueling year of disease, death, racial strife, street violence, economic collapse and political discord the likes of which have not been seen in the United States in years, they may look back on this day as a pivotal juncture."

Two days later, I authorized the Wesley to vaccinate my mom. Nurse Amy was one of the first Saratogians to get the shot, two actually so that she'd have the maximum protection possible. The Federal government left the bulk of the vaccination effort up to the states, but nursing homes were prioritized to receive the first doses of the vaccine. To do this as quickly as possible, the Federal government partnered with large chain drug stores and gave the vaccine to local pharmacists to administer these shots.

To many of us, the launch of this vaccination effort gave us hope that we might finally be in a position to stop the virus. I thought getting my mom vaccinated could speed up our reunion and bring an end to the policies that isolated her from us. The trouble was the virus had a head start, not only in the US, but inside the Wesley too.

My mom was one of the nicest people you could meet and the consummate caregiver, but now she pushed, hit, and yelled at other residents and staff with regularity. When she and the others were allowed to gather together and to walk the halls, sometimes Nurse Amy in-

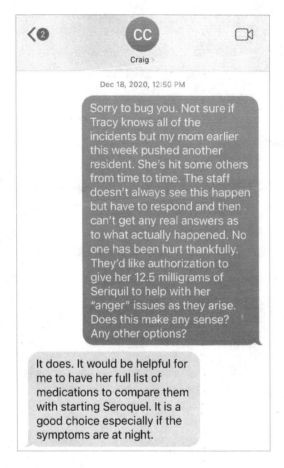

structed them on what to do or where to go and they didn't listen. Other times, the hallways could become congested and my mom never liked to wait in traffic.

The Wesley was required to call me after every incident. She punched staff members, threw things across the cafeteria, and had to be physically removed from a room several times as she was deemed a threat to herself and others. With each call, the only thing I could do was apologize and then hope everyone was okay and understood this was the disease and this situation, not my mom.

When the trauma of the situation or her Alzheimer's got the best of her, there were a select few staff members that she trusted who were asked to intervene. The strategy that worked best for them was to take her to a quiet place and listen to her explain as best she could what was wrong. This was exactly what I did when I was allowed to visit, and as her physical and mental health declined my presence would have helped even more.

She now also fell more frequently, and was unable to communicate how she ended up on the ground or if she was in pain and where it hurt. As they tried to investigate, the Wesley officially called her a "limited historian" due to her dementia and her inability to help them figure out what really happened.

As December came to a close and I was not allowed to visit, my mom's nurse felt some additional medication might calm her down, and allow her to sleep better too. I texted this suggestion to Craig and he recommended we give it a try. There was nothing else we could do to save her from the loneliness, anger, sadness, pain, isolation, anxiety, and frustration she must have felt.

Tracy Shimkus Cheifetz
Dec 25, 2020

So many years we spent Christmas Day in the car...driving from MA to VA. Today was (all things considered) a nice day. Got to spend time with family over the Portal (that included my Mom for a quick visit... albeit too quick), opened gifts (and I think I was the big winner this year!), ate a wonderful meal together - all 5 of us, and even played a few games. It was short (Jared came home from the firehouse around 10am and heads back around 5pm), but very sweet! Hope everyone else made the most of it!

There was little joy this Christmas. Ben and Katie decided it was not safe to join us in Saratoga. It was quiet, surreal. Lisa and I never bought a tree, nor did she even decorate our home as usual. No kids, Christmas jammies, family adventures, or presents to open.

All of us had twenty minutes for a virtual visit with our mom. She was in her room and I could see that the door to the hallway was open. When we wished her a Merry Christmas, she said: "I didn't know it was Christmas." Neither did we, really; it was just maddening to see what this virus did to our lives.

In a column published before the New Year, I had a message to share with everyone. Once again, I included a photo of my mom, the one with her and her dog from March 12th when we were last together.

"The heroes at the Wesley have been amazing. But under New York's protocols, no one from our family has been able to sit with my mom without a mask, to give her a hug, to hold her hand, or to share a cup of coffee and a chocolate chip cookie with her in 281 straight days - - not on her birthday, Mother's Day, Thanksgiving, or Christmas."

"I'm sharing this story because we're starting to see the distribution of vaccines that can stop the spread of this virus. Saying yes to get vaccinated will help us to save our local businesses, to keep our schools open, to see our favorite local attractions come to life again, and to put local people back to work. Saying yes will make it possible for me and my family to visit in person with my mom and to give her a hug again. So if you are at all on the fence on whether or not to get vaccinated, please look at the photo of my mom, Amy Shimkus, on this page. She will get vaccinated as soon as possible and so will I. We hope you will too!"

JANUARY 1, 2021

ONE YEAR AGO, on New Year's Day, the World Health Organization (WHO) had some difficult questions for officials in Wuhan, China about a cluster of cases of pneumonia. Three months later, the WHO declared that this COVID-19 virus was a global pandemic. The world had not experienced such a devastating public health challenge in a century.

In 2020, more than 1.8 million people around the world died after they contracted this virus. The death toll in the US now surpassed 350,000 people. Nearly 40,000 New York residents were dead. So many more suffered or were scared, stressed, alone and tired.

Now there was a glimmer of hope. By January 1, 2021, there were two vaccines approved for use and a third was on the way. Nearly 3 million Americans had already received one dose of the vaccine. Millions more were eager to get the shot, but so far vaccine supplies were severely limited. The virus had the upper hand as the New Year began. Nowhere did we see this more than right here in Saratoga.

The Wesley had taken every possible precaution. It didn't matter—once the virus found a way into Wesley, it wreaked havoc. Thirteen residents died between November and the end of 2020. In the first ten days of 2021, seven more residents perished.

Every time a staff member or resident tested positive or died, I got a text message. Still, the texts never scared me, if only because I figured that if my mom contracted the virus I'd get a personal call instead.

"I spent Christmas morning working on personal notes to family members of residents we lost," one employee shared with me. "It was so discouraging to all of us. We had done everything possible to keep the virus out. It was just really depressing."

Residents and employees were tested twice a week. The employees went to the hospital testing center, while the residents were tested by staff. I imagined this process was a challenge, especially in a memory care unit. Some residents were non-verbal. Others, like my mom, could get agitated. None understood why someone wanted to stick a swab up both of their nostrils twice a week.

My mom never tested positive and never had the virus. The staff on my mom's floor kept the virus from invading this space. "I honestly think it is because of that one positive case the first weekend of November that was asymptomatic and maybe a false positive," Tracy surmised. "Mom's floor has been full PPE ever since because of the type of care needed there. Hopefully all residents on her floor were given the vaccine the other week so they will get the second round on January 12th. They are now saying full immunity of 95% is achieved two weeks from getting the second dose. Her floor needs to make it to January 26th!!!"

On January 4th, we learned that a new, more deadly variant that originated in the United Kingdom, was detected for the first time in the United States, right here in Saratoga. With International travel largely banned, no one knew how it got here. Those who did travel had to test negative before they could leave the UK and after they arrived in the U.S. Yet, once again, the virus didn't care what protocols we put in place. It spread wherever it wanted.

Governor Cuomo personally announced the discovery of this new variant live on television. He shared with the world that a 62-year old man from Saratoga was the first person in the US to test positive for the UK variant, but did not publicly name him. He did, however, name the store where he worked; N. Fox Jewelers, in downtown Saratoga. I knew immediately that it was Harvey Fox, a co-owner of the store with his wife Cassie.

"ABC World News must have mentioned Saratoga six times," Tracy told me. "They even had Cuomo saying the 62-year-old man has symptoms but is doing better. Hope you and Lisa haven't been jewelry shopping lately." My cousin Jen texted me: "I see your city is the unfortunate one to have the new strain. Stay safe."

I texted both of them back: "I know the owners very well. Harvey practiced social distancing before it was a thing. He stopped shaking hands years ago and has always been super careful. I can't believe he caught the virus. He's okay thankfully."

The Saratoga Crew immediately heard from hotels and restaurants who reported canceled reservations. My dentist shared that patients were so freaked out that they canceled appointments. A local optometrist and a chiropractor reported the same. A local restaurant owner emailed me, angered because the Chamber didn't call for the city to close down.

"This is directed at you and everyone else working at the Chamber. How can you morally justify promoting happy hours, specials and indoor dining while watching your neighbors die, fall gravely ill and suffer through a horrible, highly contagious illness? 'Save Our Locals' ...? What a farce. Your locals are sick and dying. If you and others aren't innovative enough to figure this out, I call for new leadership. How many more Saratogians must fall ill and die before you stop encouraging people to go out to eat? When (if ever) we make it through this, the actions (and inactions) of the Chamber leadership will not be forgotten. What a tragedy."

The owners of the jewelry store never traveled to the UK. Online, however, people heard the Governor and saw photos of the store and accused them of putting our community at risk. Months later, I learned that the Governor knew that Harvey had this variant of the virus before they did. Forty-five minutes before Cuomo's press conference, an epidemiologist with the state's lab called Harvey to share his test results and to let him know that Cuomo planned to make an announcement momentarily.

Eventually, the state health department traced the variant to the daughter of one of the store's employees. She and her boyfriend were in the UK. They came home to spend time with family for Christmas, and followed all of the protocols and never tested positive. While several store employees got sick, no one who worked there or was a customer died. The same was unfortunately not true for another local business owner.

After the New Year, the owner of Saratoga Guitar caught the virus and died at home. "It is with great sadness that the Saratoga Springs Downtown Business Association Board must say goodbye to our good friend, Matt McCabe," began an email from Deann to all DBA members.

Matt was the first person I knew that was killed by the virus. As I explained to the restaurant owner who called for us to shut down the city, the Chamber and the Saratoga Crew absolutely understood the crisis we faced. But rather than a shut down, what we really needed was the state to set up a local vaccination clinic. That was the only way to stop the spread of this new variant and to protect our neighbors, friends and families.

In response to the discovery of the UK variant, New York State set up a special pop-up testing facility in the Saratoga Spa State Park. State officials declared that anyone that was a customer of N. Fox Jewelers was invited to get tested. Hundreds showed up, way more than had been in the store.

Saratoga now had nearly 3,000 active cases, and this number would soon climb to over 4,000. Thousands more were required to quarantine, and we had no idea if this was caused by Holiday gatherings or the new variant.

Since the Governor went to great lengths to share with the world that this new variant was here, I thought it was time for him to do more than just set up a testing site. At this point, the Governor had opened thirteen mass vaccination sites. They were located hours away from Saratoga. We had the perfect location for a new state run mass vaccination site, the Saratoga Springs City Center.

On January 5, 2021, I released a statement: "Saratoga has a motto: Health. History. Horses. In Saratoga, HEALTH comes first. We wish our friends affected by the latest development well. We know they are doing everything they can to put health first. The same is true for all of our local and county officials. New York State is helping with more testing and contact tracing. However, if we are going to put HEALTH first, we need to get more vaccinations into the arms of more people. We need a local vaccination site in Saratoga. We, in collaboration with our community partners, are ready to help."

State Senator Daphne Jordan, Congresswoman Elise Stefanik, and Assemblywoman Carrie Woerner all amplified the Chamber's call to action. Our original Tweet was viewed by 50,000 people in twenty four hours. I did interviews on all of the local stations. We emailed our statement to thousands of people. The local demand for access to a vaccine was significant and this call to action gathered local support quickly.

The Saratoga County Board of Supervisors designated the City Center as their mass vaccination site. The County paid the City Center so they'd be ready to host a mass vaccination event. Volunteers from local fire departments were ready to administer the shots, and the Saratoga Crew lined up sponsors to finance any unexpected costs. But not one shot was ever administered in the City Center - the state repeatedly said no to our request.

The state's vaccine roll out did not go smoothly. There was no coordination by the state with local county or city leaders anywhere. In Saratoga, our county public health department had the ability to quickly start up a vaccination effort at 17 separate locations, 18 if we counted the City Center. This would have made getting vaccinated far more convenient, likely increasing the number who decided to get the shot. Instead, the Governor limited the distribution of most of the state's supply of vaccines to his state-run sites.

I called this "The Hunger Games" as it became a competition to get the shot. This strategy pitted every eligible resident against one another. The first challenge was the state's online vaccine appointment system. The limited number of appointments possible at these sites were gone in minutes. Those who hit refresh on their screen or used multiple devices were the most likely to win an appointment, not those with comorbidities or most at risk.

If you got an appointment, you now needed time off and transportation to the state run sites. Friends of mine who got an appointment drove two or more hours each way to sites in Utica, Syracuse,

Potsdam or Plattsburgh. Of the first 600,000 people vaccinated in New York, state records showed that one quarter traveled more than 2 hours. Only those with computer access, time, a car, and money could get these first vaccine shots.

Saratoga residents had the resources to push through these obstacles. That's likely why our county consistently outperformed the state's overall vaccination rate, even without a local site. Even those Saratoga residents who did not have the means to win gained access. That's because our senior center, for instance, enlisted volunteers with computers to help people get appointments and others with cars to take them to these state-run sites.

On January 23, after my mom got her second vaccine, the Wesley took her photo. I gave them a roll of the #IGotTheShot stickers the Chamber and the Hospital printed. I asked them to give two stickers to my mom and to take a photo of her with them. We used this photo in our latest campaign to profile people who got their shot. The hope was that as people saw other people get their shot that this would inspire everyone to do the same.

Before we posted this photo, I texted it to Tracy and Trisha. Tracy responded: "I really like the picture of Mom. But, boy has she aged in the last year." Trisha texted me too: "I had a call scheduled for this morning. I just got a call from Bridgette. She said that mom is really not having a good morning. She doesn't want to leave her room right now." Now even my mom was tired of virtual visits.

On January 24, Ben was able to get his first shot. A week before, I saw the Governor announce that front-line grocery workers were now eligible. The Chamber emailed this news to local employers, and I texted Ben. As we shared vaccination protocol updates, those who couldn't get an appointment reached out to me for help.

"Todd, Can you assist my wife and I to obtain the COVID-19 vaccine? We are both over 70," the owner of a local hotel texted me. A CPA emailed me: "Todd, still trying to get my 90-year old mother scheduled for a vaccine. Any Saratoga County suggestions." A friend of mine texted: "Any chance you can help two eighty year olds to get vaccines at the City Center."

The reality is that I was never in a position to help anyone get vaccinated, not even Lisa. When teachers became eligible, Lisa rushed to complete the online process before she left school one afternoon, and later learned that she didn't hit the final confirmation button. The only thing I could do was jump online like everyone else.

"I used three devices at the same time," I texted her after I got her an appointment. "It's in three weeks in Plattsburgh, which is two hours away. This is the best I can do."

Then a week later, local school nurses teamed up with our County Public Health Department. The county allowed these nurses to use the limited vaccine doses the state gave Saratoga to open a local site just for school personnel. The site was five minutes from our house. My mom, Ben, and Lisa were now vaccinated, but Katie and I would not be eligible for weeks.

Getting vaccinated was not Katie's top priority. She wanted to find a new job first. When a friend from college heard she lost hers at MIT, he reached out and told her his organization, located in California, needed a junior copywriter. The person they hired would report directly to him. Katie got the job and started in late-January.

"You can't move to California," Lisa texted Katie. "I will miss you too much." This is when we learned that she didn't need to move. Her friend worked remotely himself, from Portland, Oregon, and they hired Katie to work from her apartment in Boston.

Prior to the pandemic, Katie would have been a long shot to get this job unless she agreed to relocate. But COVID forced many employers and employees to rethink remote work. For some, this option became preferable, a new normal. For Katie, this new job paid better, and it was a perfect match given her love of writing.

By early February, nineteen more Wesley residents died from COVID-19 which brought the total dead to 39 residents. All were killed during the second wave. To fight off the virus, the Wesley was locked down and raced to get all residents and staff vaccinated. This was the best way for everyone there to stay alive.

For months, the number of nursing home residents killed by the virus in New York was a source of conflict and controversy. The Cuomo administration consistently said about 9,000 nursing home residents died from the virus. Some of the Governor's opponents suggested the administration under-reported this data.

On January 28, New York's Attorney General released a 76-page report that accused Governor Cuomo and his COVID-19 team of under-reporting nursing home deaths by up to 50 percent. Days later, the Department of Health admitted that more than 15,000 nursing home residents had actually died in the first months of the pandemic.

Some called for Cuomo's resignation, and the families of those who perished wanted an investigation. Did state protocols contribute to the high number of deaths? Is this why the Governor under-reported the real numbers?

I wondered if this was why the nursing home visitation protocols the past summer were so restrictive. If the Governor knew the real number of deaths, it seemed reasonable to me that he'd want to do everything he could to prevent this death toll from increasing as that might cause more people to actually question his decisions.

FEBRUARY 2021

Now, I was about to find out what it felt like to be at risk and isolated. Still not yet eligible for the vaccine, I took all the necessary precautions so that I could safely go out in the community. I wore a mask, practiced social distancing, and used hand sanitizer all the time.

On Tuesday, February 9, I did all of this while several of us visited restaurants with our local media. We traveled to these businesses in separate cars to do interviews about a new promotion set to start that Thursday.

"Restaurants need help, so that's why Saratoga Eagle and Driscoll Foods are splitting the bill," read our post on the Chamber's Facebook page. "All you have to do is order out or dine in at any participating restaurant this Thursday, and you will be reimbursed 50% of your receipt total, up to $30."

The split the bill promotion worked better than we imagined. On Thursday, participants turned in receipts from 2,400 orders where they spent more than $180,000 at the 35 restaurants who participated. Some restaurants were so busy they stopped taking orders by 5 p.m.

I was scheduled to pick up dinner for Lisa and me at 5:30 p.m. But at 4:30 p.m., I got a text from one of the sponsors I was with on Tuesday. He asked me to call him right away. Online, we could monitor how many people were participating and what they were spending, so I thought he was nervous about how much this promotion might actually cost them. That was not the problem.

"Todd, I'm so sorry to do this to you," he told me. "On Wednesday I didn't feel great. I went to get tested. Today, I found out that I have COVID." He and I had sat together at the last restaurant we visited. We had food and a couple of beers together. I was a "close contact" and had to quarantine immediately.

SaratogaChamber @Saratoga... · 2/9/21 ···
Restaurants need help, so @SaratogaEagle & Driscoll Foods are splitting the bill with you! @splitthebillny this Thurs, Feb 11th! Order out or dine in at participating restau...

I stood at my desk in my office and walked myself through what I had told others to do when confronted with this situation. I packed up my laptop and some paperwork, and I stopped outside of Deb Zeman's office next to mine. "I had a close contact when we were promoting Split the Bill," I told her. "I have to quarantine for ten days. Since we have separate offices and wear masks, no one else needs to quarantine unless I test positive."

She was not stunned. Throughout the pandemic, I had been in close contact with a lot of people. If it was deemed safe, I was one of the first to go. I did this with take-out and as businesses were allowed to reopen. My job was to support these businesses and to show that you could patronize them safely. Everyone expected that my luck would eventually run out and I'd test positive.

I called Lisa, and she called the school nurse. The nurse advised her to stay as far away from me as possible. Like the Chamber staff, she didn't need to quarantine unless I became sick. I texted Ryan, Darryl and Deann as the four of us met the day before and sat at a table together. They didn't need to quarantine, but I thought they should be careful. "Oh shit," Ryan said. "That's not good," Darryl added.

I felt fine and had no symptoms. I really didn't ever think about my own health. I thought about the impact this might have on other people's lives if I did get it. It was easy for me to quarantine, but it would have been terrible if I had spread it to others. What kept me safe this time? I believe it was the fact that I kept my mask on even at the bar. My mask only came off of one ear when I took a bite or a drink. I put it back on as soon as possible.

After Tracy heard the news, she worried and called me every day to be sure I was okay. I shared the news with Katie and Ben, who were also concerned and checked in from time to time. Everyone at the Chamber was informed, and they dropped a supply of coffee and beer off on my front porch to hold me over.

No one from the County ever called me to make sure I quarantined. Because they didn't call, I didn't share this news with anyone else. I didn't want to explain the details of my exposure to anyone, nor did I want people to feel afraid of being with me in the future.

Everyone that knew I was quarantined joked that the virus wouldn't kill me, but the boredom of being stuck at home for ten days might. Craig told me it was okay for me to run outside as long as I was alone, and I did that every morning. Rather than sending me to the store or a restaurant to pick things up, Lisa ordered the items or food we needed and did curbside delivery. I definitely didn't like my time in isolation, but I was never bored.

Stuck at home, I had plenty of time to engage in another fight. This time, I wanted the New York State legislature to pass a Caregiver's Bill of Rights. "Seems simple. Allow every family member with a loved one in a nursing home to designate one person to be allowed access," I tweeted in support of this bill.

In other states, similar laws allowed a designated caregiver to visit their loved ones in a nursing home, provided they followed the same precautions as the employees. Had such a law been in place in New York, I would have been able to visit my mom regularly most of the last year. With his extraordinary executive powers, Governor Cuomo could have approved such a policy on his own, but he never did.

Even now, after the Legislature approved the caregiver's bill, in late-February, he initially refused to sign it into law. Cuomo had thirty days to act. He took every one of them before he did anything as vaccinated nursing home residents remained in isolation. We'd get to see my mom before the Governor ever signed this legislation, but it would not be the reunion I hoped for all this time.

On my fourth day in quarantine, Ben called to let me know that Joey Gugliemeli, aka Sherry Pie, was scheduled to "come clean" on the

Tamron Hall Show. This talk show's social media called him a "breakout star." They never once invited Joey's victims to share their stories, and they neglected to tell their followers that he admitted to sexually harassing more than twenty people nearly one year ago.

After a little research, I found the Twitter account for Candi Carter, a producer of this show, and I sent her a direct message. "My son, Ben Shimkus is one of the people Sherry abused. He's already reliving that trauma. Please believe the victims and cancel this appearance."

Three hours later, she messaged me back, and I sent her Ben's cell number. In my reply, I added: "Ben was the brave first person that brought Sherry's long history of abuse to the public eye. You can call him."

A producer eventually called Ben, and he taped the conversation. "We want to fix this," this person said. Ben responded that the only way to "fix this" was to cancel Joey's appearance. He explained that the victims were ready to take his place. The producer countered, as if this were a negotiation, and invited Ben to submit a video, which he did. They never aired it.

Like RuPaul a year ago, Tamron Hall didn't care about the victims. In quarantine, I watched this unfold, and learned a lot about the plight of victims. Joey got a television platform to share more lies while Ben again was attacked on social media. People accused him of seeking fame and fortune. They suggested that if the accusations were true that Ben and the other victims should have gone to the police. The worst suggested the victims deserved the abuse for being so naive and falling for Joey's ruse.

Very soon, the world watched as a different group of victims came forward. They accused their boss, also an Emmy-winning celebrity, with violating New York's workplace sexual harassment laws. This person had a substantial platform, lots of power, and a desire to remain in power. This leader, his enablers, and fans would soon attack these brave victims too.

MARCH 2021

IN DECEMBER, a former aide to Governor Cuomo accused him of sexual harassment in a Tweet. She said he had kissed her against her will. "It's just not true," he said. In an effort to discredit her, his office attempted to leak her personnel files to the media. In February via a blog post, she eventually told more of her story and only then did the traditional media take notice.

Three days later, a second former employee came forward to accuse the Governor of sexual harassment. "I understood that the governor wanted to sleep with me," she told the New York Times. "I felt horribly uncomfortable and scared." When this first happened, she followed state protocols and reported the specifics of her complaint to the Governor's chief of staff. A week later, she was transferred to another state job and no disciplinary action was taken.

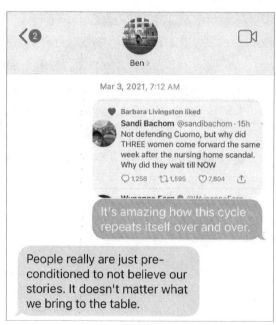

Supporters and fans of the Governor went after these victims immediately even as more came forward. "Not defending Cuomo, but why did these women come forward the same week after the nursing home scandal. Why did they wait till NOW?"

Others added: What they experienced wasn't sexual harassment. They should have ran out of the room. They should have known better. They put themselves in that position. Why didn't they go to the police? These were the same comments Ben received as people undermined his case so they could minimize the damage to the star they adored.

The Governor ignored the calls for him to resign. In his quest to survive, his fight-or-flight reflex led him first to defend himself and later to attack these victims. Legislative leaders launched an investigation, as did New York's Attorney General. But even if they ultimately believed the victims and found he did something wrong, I expected the Governor to remain in office. He had too much power to be overthrown.

On March 10, 2021 as I worked late in my office, my cell phone rang and I noticed the call was from my mom's nurse. "Hi Todd, I'm calling to let you know that your mom fell," she told me. "She tripped and we think she broke her hip. She was in a lot of pain so we took her to Saratoga Hospital's emergency room."

After I hung up, I ran out of my office and raced to the emergency room. The people at the front desk initially refused to let me in to see her. Visitation was restricted and there was nothing they could do. I was polite and calmly walked outside to contact the Hospital President.

There was no way, with her Alzheimer's, that she could advocate for herself. I needed to be there to authorize any procedure they needed to do. "We do visitation if there is a reason," the President told me. I went back in and was now allowed to enter the emergency room. I was so focused on finding my mom to be sure she was okay that I didn't think about how she might respond and whether or not she might recognize me.

It had been 363 days since I last saw my mom in person.

I slowed my pace as I approached her room. I didn't want to run in and startle her. Carefully I pushed open the door and peeked my head in first. No one else was there but my mom. Her bed was in the middle of the room, angled so that she was nearly sitting up. She was alert, awake and surprisingly calm.

"Hi Todd. Boy am I glad you're here," she said as soon as she saw my face. She looked pale, and her hair was so long. I walked over and gave her a hug. I had no idea if this was allowed; I didn't care at this point. I suspected she needed one. I know I did.

After the hug, I stepped back a little, just to be safe. "How are you?" I asked and she started to talk, but she was unable to tell me what happened or if she was hurt. Instead, I told her the nurses thought she broke her hip. When I asked if it hurt, she said no.

A doctor came into her room, and I put Craig on speakerphone to translate doctorese for me. They both agreed that surgery was required as soon as the next day. Throughout this time, my mom didn't complain about anything. She seemed perfectly fine, until they tried to move her. No one was ready for her reaction. The trauma of having lived in isolation with Alzheimer's, and now a broken hip, unleashed a side of my mom no one ever saw before.

Unable to escape, my mom fought with us whenever she was in pain. I watched as she tried to hit the nurses, CNAs, a security guard, and even me. On multiple occasions, she tried to pull out her IV and to bite us when we reached out to stop her. My mom even managed to kick her feet, both of them. How she did this with a broken hip is beyond me. She swore and yelled at us. One time when I tried to restrain one of her arms, she nearly broke my fingers as she squeezed them with her other hand.

This happened every time they had to move her. I learned to keep a pillow near me which I used to cover up and hold down her left arm where the IV was without hurting her. I doubt the hospital staff generally allowed a non-medical, non-staff relative to participate in restraints, but they really had no choice. It took three or four of us each time until the pain medication they gave sedated her.

The worst fight took place the next morning right before her surgery. I went with her as they wheeled her down to the surgical unit without incident. Then as I stood by her bed, I watched as she stopped looking at me and her eyes started to scan the room. Unable to see a way out, she prepared to fight again. I warned everyone, but no one there anticipated her strength.

"I want to go home!" she yelled as she tried to pull out the IV. She hit one of the nurses with her hand, hard enough that the nurse had to step away. My mom then easily removed the IV and grabbed a stethoscope from another nurse. She swung it at all of us and we all had to duck. This is when I stepped away so I didn't get hurt.

Besides the pillow, I learned to keep my cell phone close. When she was upset, I played the video of Lisa, Katie, Ben and me singing, "You Will Be Found." She was in no condition to watch the video, but she listened to the music. It had calmed her down the night before so much so that the nurse wrote "loves the song you will be found," on a white board in her room. This time, I turned it up as loud as I could and played the song over and over.

"Even when the dark comes crashing through. When you need a friend to carry you. When you're broken on the ground. You will be found." The song was oddly prophetic, eerily accurate. She had fallen and broken her hip. I ran to the hospital and stayed with her nearly the entire time. Now as she entered surgery after the nurses regained control, I was glad Tracy was on the way to Saratoga to help me too.

My mom's physical progress was slow after the surgery. It was days before she was released from the hospital. Whenever she was in pain, she continued to fight. Unfortunately, Tracy experienced these fights too and they were no less difficult for her to watch. When my mom wanted to go home, a team effort and some music were required to stabilize the situation.

Tracy and I talked openly about the trauma and stress this caused us and our mom. Craig told her to stay as long as she needed. Lisa asked me repeatedly, "Are you okay?" Tracy and I both admitted that while we sat with her and she rested that we prayed for God, or anyone really, to rescue her and let her pass peacefully. We hated watching our mom in pain, angry, and confused.

One night, I whispered to my mom that it was okay if she went home. I promised her we'd all be okay and she didn't need to worry about us anymore. We loved her and didn't want her to suffer, not from being alone because of COVID-19 or from the steady decline in her health because of Alzheimer's.

Her physical decline was obvious. The mental toll of the isolation and Alzheimer's was almost as clear. During one of their first visits, my mom started to tell Tracy a story and she never stopped talking. "I felt like she was telling me everything that happened to her this past year. I'm not sure what was real. It was so sad to think that she had no one to talk to this way for so long. I just listened and tried not to cry."

On March 17, my mom went back to the Wesley. It came with a promise from the Wesley that I was now approved for compassionate care visits every day. Everyone at the Hospital and Wesley believed it was vital for her safety and care for me to be there, provided I took and passed a COVID test every day on site before I entered the facility.

Tracy said goodbye at the hospital. She gave Mom a hug and told her she loved her. She did the same to me. "I couldn't have done this without you," I told her. "This was an exhausting ordeal for all of us," Tracy wrote on Facebook. "A year is a long time to be separated from everyone you know, everyone you love, especially when you are suffering from Alzheimer's. My mom received a warm welcome back by the incredible staff at the Wesley and I am so comforted by this."

As our mom was brought back to the Wesley, Trisha learned her blood work showed no more signs of cancer. "So many blessings today, thank you all for your prayers and help," she said on Facebook.

If my mom had not broken her hip, we still would have been separated, unable to be together ten days later. Nursing home residents in New York had to be traumatized or near death for a family member to be allowed to visit. Yet on March 22, one of the Governor's advisors had the audacity to say publicly, "We have already taken steps to expand visitation." She said this in response to a question about why the Governor had not yet signed the caretakers bill passed by the legislature nearly a month before. I responded to Beth and the Governor on Twitter, "I just want everyone to know that Beth Garvey has no idea what she's talking about."

The Wesley scheduled my compassionate care visit every day at 10 a.m. First, I had to put on a surgical mask in my car. After I walked into the Wesley, I stepped up to a machine that took my temperature. Then, I was directed to take a pen out of a cup marked "clean," and I used it to fill out a report where I indicated the date and time of my visit; my name, address, phone number and email; as well as who I planned to visit, and where in the facility. The pen was then placed in a cup marked "dirty."

A nurse was there and she tore open a little packet to remove a cotton swab and a COVID test kit. After she completed the COVID test, I gave her my cell phone number and went back to my car. Fifteen minutes later, she called to tell me that it was safe for me to visit. If I wanted to visit my mom, this is the protocol I was required to follow every day. No other family members were allowed to visit, unless their loved-one was near death.

In the final hours before the deadline, the Governor signed the caretakers bill. It was only then that everyone else could visit their loved-ones, and I could visit without a daily test. Later in the year, this law kept us together as a new variant attacked. But right now, what I really needed was to get vaccinated so the two of us could visit safely.

All of us in the Saratoga Crew learned a lot about each other this past year. Maybe too much. Ryan will die if he eats fish. Darryl doesn't like to sit in the sun. Deann has a crush on a local CEO who shall remain nameless. Shelby had washed dishes by hand for two years. Samantha's dad wanted to name her Sarah, so people like us would not call her Sam.

One of the things they learned about me is that I have a debilitating fear of needles. Just the thought of a blood test or shot, and I get anxious, turn white, and start to sweat. Many times, I passed

out after I got a shot, and sometimes I had a seizure. I believe my fear of needles goes back to the surgeries and trauma when I was born.

But now I was leading the I Got the Shot campaign to encourage people to get vaccinated. My mom was featured in this promotion, and I told everyone repeatedly that I planned to get the shot when I was eligible. So I knew I had to practice what I preached. It was also clear to me that if I was vaccinated that it would be safer for me to visit my mom. As so many things had been this year, my decision to get vaccinated as soon as possible was both personal and a part of my job.

By the time Governor Cuomo announced that any resident aged fifty or older was eligible, the hunger games competition to get vaccinated was over. The supply of doses had increased significantly. There were also more sites where you could get the shot. I got mine at a Walgreens less than a half-mile from my office.

To stay calm, I needed something to do to keep my mind off of the needle. When I arrived, they gave me paperwork to fill out and told me to take a seat. I sat down; checked emails and texted a couple of people. Then I heard the pharmacist say my name.

I stood up and walked quickly toward him, and never made eye contact. "I have a fear of needles," I said immediately. "Please don't tell me anything. Just do it as fast as you can." I sat down with my right shoulder facing him and looked the other way. He wiped my arm with something wet and then I felt a slight pinch. "We're all done," he said.

For many, there was relief when they got the shot, and they believed this protected them from the virus. Everyone who got vaccinated hoped that they would then be able to do the things they had been prevented from doing for so long. For me, at least at first, I was excited that I didn't pass out. Three weeks later, I got the second shot again without incident.

APRIL 2021

By April 1, 2021, COVID-19 had killed more than 2.8 million people across the world. The first wave hit New York the hardest in March and April of 2020. In the winter of 2021, the entire country endured a far more significant surge, worse than anyone predicted. The number of deaths in the US alone now stood at 550,000.

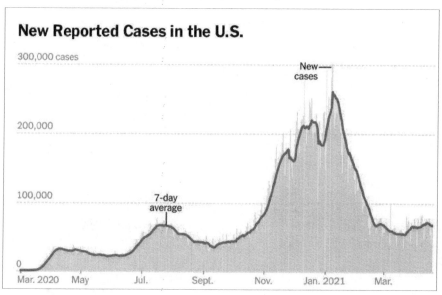

The good news, or so we thought, was that one in five or 66 million Americans were now fully vaccinated. Another 46 million Americans had at least one dose. On average, three million doses were administered per day in the US. Those who were vaccinated felt free again, and safe to gather with loved ones no matter where they lived. Not everyone, however, planned to get vaccinated and this would soon derail our hope that the pandemic was over.

The CDC said it was safe for fully vaccinated family members to gather together again. So on April 6, my mom was reunited with her sisters Joanie and Betty as they all were vaccinated. Betty had not seen my mom in 14 months, while Joanie had not seen my mom since Christmas Eve in 2019.

My mom was confined to a wheelchair and was still occasionally in pain. She had trouble when she tried to stand up. I wasn't sure she got as much physical therapy as she needed, but on most days when I visited she was comfortable and safe. She did better when she had people there to listen to her stories and to spend time with her. Joanie painted my mom's nails during this visit. I was still trying to get her scheduled for a haircut, but there was a huge backlog of people that wanted this as well.

"We had a great visit," Joanie texted. "It was great being able to give her a hug and kiss and to see her in person. It was a nice day." She also sent me some photos. The picture of my mom and Joanie as they sat side by side with their heads together was the best. There was pure joy on that day and in that photo.

Governor Cuomo was not joyful. He visited state run vaccination centers where he hosted near daily briefings again. As he faced continued scrutiny, he used this platform to show he was still in charge. On April 9, he declared that all New Yorkers age 16 and older were now eligible for the vaccine. On April 12, he announced he planned to provide vaccines to college students so they could get vaccinated before they traveled home for the summer.

At no point did he announce an end to the myriad of restrictions he put in place that impacted so many parts of our lives and businesses. Now instead, he offered us what seemed like a haphazard partial return to normal that allowed him to extend his power for what seemed like an eternity. Effective April 19, he lifted the state's curfew for bars and restaurants. Then on April 26, he authorized museums, zoos, and movie theaters to increase their capacity limits to fifty percent. Why 50%? None of this made sense.

By April 11, the Saratoga County Public Health Department had recorded more than 14,000 positive cases since the start of the pandemic. 159 local residents were killed by the virus during this time. But as was the case in the rest of the US, it appeared the vaccines had helped us to gain the upper hand in this war with the virus.

To continue to encourage people to get the shot, the Chamber now created and shared a Saratoga COVID-19 vaccination chart. We released this chart on this day to celebrate that 100,000 Saratogians had managed to get at least one dose of a vaccine. The chart made it easy for everyone to see the progress we made locally.

"We're starting to see local customers return," a local restaurant owner told me. "They share with us right away that they were recently vaccinated and how excited they are to be back. We are filling up our tables again."

Lisa's school year went better than expected too as they never needed to shut down, nor did she have to teach virtually. Lisa never got sick and neither did her students. Her students were in class with her every day, and they wore masks without protest. This was not the case everywhere.

"The only time I have to talk to my students about masks is when they sneeze," Lisa told me. "I then walk over to them and hand them a new mask. I tell them to either throw the other one away or to bring it home to be washed if it's a cloth one."

Her students were like the grandchildren we didn't have. She tested them at the start of the year. They were all behind grade level. Lisa did her best to help them catch up. She made learning fun and safe. She created "Mellon Headz" for all of her students, herself and the principal. Each was an illustrated figure she customized that looked just like the real person. These illustrations were copied, cut, laminated and affixed to the students desk and locker. She used them on her website where she shared resources with parents so they could help their children too. It was a fun way for everyone to see the people behind the masks. One of her students drew one of her. Lisa made it her Facebook profile picture.

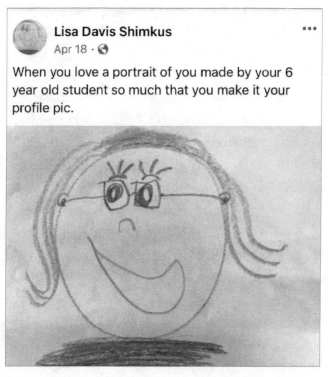

"I think that's a very nice compliment when a student draws you. Actually, a huge compliment. You must provide a loving and supportive classroom to your students. Cheers," a neighbor commented. "Yay! First grade is great. Lots of work but worth every minute," another teacher said. Lisa replied to everyone, "I absolutely love it. I'm exhausted but I'm having so much fun."

On my mom's 77th birthday, Lisa and I were with her to celebrate. Tracy, Trisha, Joanie and Betty were there virtually on our portal. This year we had two hours to spend with her. I brought her a bag of gifts, which included a birthday tiara, a new stuffed animal dog, cards, and a box of chocolate chip cookies. I took each gift out of the bag and explained what it was and who it was from. She smiled as she held each one, and wore the tiara all day.

"We can tell that your mom is comforted when you are here," her nurse told me. "Six months ago, your mom started losing weight and cried a lot. Now she doesn't cry as much, and she's even gained a little weight. Your visits are very helpful."

Tracy, Trisha and I posted birthday photos on social media. Having opportunities again to be with my mom was tremendously uplifting, not just for her but for all of us. In many ways, this joy masked the continued decline in her ability to communicate caused by her Alzheimer's. But having been separated for so long, we focused on enjoying the moments we were together.

Two weeks later, I asked her to sing happy birthday to Ben. She sat in her recliner and I told her that I would count to three and then she could sing. Instead of singing the song, she repeated what I said, "one, two, three," and then said "want me to do that again?" I responded, "sure then say happy birthday Ben." This time, she looked right at the camera with a big smile and said: "happy birthday Ben, yea!"

One year ago, she sang happy birthday to me for Tracy on a video she recorded virtually and without much coaching. Now she couldn't remember the words to the song. More and more, my mom made up words. A few times, I would repeat the fake word she just said and with a laugh ask if she could spell that for me. Today, I just told her that she did a great job when she wished Ben a happy birthday and that he would love it.

MAY 2021

My mom was determined to walk again. To do this safely, she needed to use a walker. This helped with her balance and minimized the chance of her tripping again. She never objected to this, but we needed to constantly remind her to do so. Often as I arrived, I'd see her in the living room or cafeteria, but I had to look for her walker so we could take a walk together.

Her friend Judy remained a loyal, near constant companion, as they sat across from each other at all meals. They often sat side by side in the living room too, and I occasionally found her in Judy's room where they watched television. Judy was always excited to see me, and I always tried to engage the two of them in conversations. "I love your mom," Judy told me one day. "She's very nice. You are too."

Besides several stuffed animals that came and went, my mom occasionally had a baby doll in her arms or on her bed. It was amazing, scary sometimes, to see how real these seemed to her. When my mom saw a doll in someone's room, she often was upset. "He's too young to sleep there alone," she told me.

Lisa and I were with her on Mother's Day. We had so much fun that I almost forgot to take a picture. We went for a walk in the corridors and sat in her room to enjoy some cookies. My sisters visited with her virtually while we were there. It felt triumphant for us to be together on this day and for her to be able to stand up by herself.

"I have been thinking about you two," my mom's best friend from nursing school commented when she saw the photo Lisa took of my mom and me. "She looks so happy to have you there. Glad you are together this year."

Just a few days later, Trisha and our mom were reunited. "It's been since February of 2020 since I last saw you," Trisha posted a day

before her visit. "My whole life I have never gone this long without you coming to see me or me coming to you. So with everything you have done for me I am coming to see you tomorrow."

Trisha brought her a white stuffed cat. This cat was perched on her brown chair when I visited the next day. Trisha still had some lingering health issues. But like our mom, she was a fighter. My mom fought to walk, and Trisha fought to reunite with our mom. She would journey back to Saratoga two weeks later, and this time she brought Tyler to see his Mimi.

One day after Trisha's visit, we all got a big surprise. While I didn't like to wear a mask, I knew from listening to the hospital's COVID-19 team that wearing masks worked. That's why I was shocked when I heard the CDC say, "Fully vaccinated people can stop wearing masks."

This announcement was made on a Thursday, and I immediately began to receive calls, emails and text messages from employers who asked: "What does this mean in New York?" Later that day, Governor Cuomo said he needed time to review this new information. But his unwillingness to adopt the CDC's recommendation immediately created a challenge for local businesses.

"You can't imagine how stressful this has been," a restaurant owner told me Friday night. "We had customers refusing to put on masks. We had others that walked out because not everyone was wearing them. We didn't know what to do."

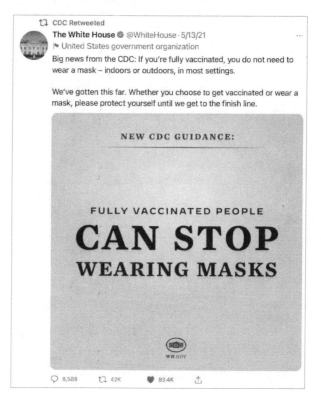

It wasn't until Monday that the Governor declared New York would follow the CDC's guidance. This helped but still there was no way to know who was vaccinated and who was not. Technically, the CDC said those who were not vaccinated needed to continue to wear a mask, but now no one did.

Looking around a day later, you'd think everyone was vaccinated because few people wore a mask. Our vaccination rate in Saratoga was now around sixty percent. So from what I could see, four out of ten people in Saratoga were not doing what the CDC recommended.

The Shimkus family didn't need to wear masks when we gathered anymore, as the four of us were fully vaccinated by early May. Katie and Ben journeyed to reunite with us after Mother's Day. This time, they stayed with us rather than in a hotel. Ben and Lisa shopped for plants, while Katie and I went out for a beer.

Ben shared that he had auditioned by video for a musical, for the first time in more than a year. "It just felt good to be preparing to audition and to perform again." Katie told us she was making more money now than ever before in her new job, so she bought a new bike.

Katie and Ben went with me to visit Grammy Amy. Ben had not seen her in three years, and the last time Katie visited with her was Christmas Day, in 2019. My mom now held a pink rabbit instead of her dog. She told the three of us that he was very soft and required all of us to pet her rabbit. Later in the year while I edited this book, I noticed that this pink rabbit was the stuffed animal she first held in our Leap of Kindness Day photo. Like my mom, this rabbit survived the isolation too.

"It's fascinating to listen to her," Katie shared as we left. "Her speech patterns are exactly like I remember. She sounds exactly like Grammy Amy. Even her tone and facial expressions are the same. But the words are all jumbled. It's almost like she was reading a Mad Lib where random words suddenly appeared in normal sentences." Leave it to Katie to best describe what it was now like to have a conversation with my mom.

SUMMER 2021

AS THE SCHOOL YEAR ENDED, Lisa's students all tested at or above grade level. None ever tested positive for the virus. They were healthy and ready for second grade. They all liked school and their teacher. Being in person made a real positive difference. Those students in other schools that were unfortunately stuck in a hybrid situation likely fell further behind. Everyone at St Mary's was ready to celebrate.

On June 5, nearly one hundred teachers, administrators, and parents gathered for the parent prom. Lisa was finally honored as the 2020 Teacher of the Year. She bought a new dress and I wore a suit - without a tie. When she was invited to say a few words, she called her speech the ABC's of teaching. Each letter was used to thank someone else or a special group of people at the school.

Two letters stood out to me. "S is for students," Lisa said. "Ahh, the students. The reason I wake up most mornings before my alarm goes off at 5:00 a.m. The reason I laugh, and the reason my hair is white. T is for teachers. My peers, friends, mentors and mental health providers. This has been a ridiculous year. You all constantly amaze me with your dedication, sacrifice and strength as we greet our kids each day with a happy good morning and a smile behind our masks."

Finally, New York celebrated on June 15. Seventy percent of all New Yorkers now had at least one vaccination shot. This was the arbitrary baseline Governor Cuomo had set for all COVID-19 restrictions to be eliminated. At his direction, taxpayer funded firework displays were held across New York to mark this achievement.

The lifting of all restrictions meant Saratoga's 2021 summer season was a full go. The Track, SPAC, Live Nation, the Casino, our bars, shops and restaurants could fully reopen. There were no capacity restrictions, no mask mandates and no social distancing requirements. In numerous interviews, I told reporters that we anticipated a "return to the Roaring 20's in Saratoga." Everyone laughed, but I was right.

Visitors and residents came back to Saratoga and our downtown in droves to have a good time. Some had too much fun, and others were just angry at how our lives were disrupted. This led to conflicts and fights, particularly in our bar district. "It's only a matter of time before something really bad is going to happen," one owner told me.

Early Saturday morning, June 26, a shot was fired. An illegal ghost gun was found. No one was hit by the shot, but someone was stabbed. The police were investigating and asked for the public's help. That was all that needed to be said. But Commissioner Dalton, now a candidate for Mayor, hosted a press conference, where she added: "It is vital that we commit to our police department not just money but with community support."

The assistant chief spoke next, not about the investigation, but instead to denounce protesters who had again called for an investigation into Darryl Mount's death. At one point, he paused and looked away from his script as the room stayed quiet. He tapped his fingers hard on the table multiple times, then said: "I'm pissed off. It is time for the silent majority to stand up and be heard. We are not a racist police department. You're either with us or you're not. DBA, Chamber, Discover Saratoga, City Center, step up."

Even though we were called out, no one from the media reached out to us for a response. The next day, I met with the Mayor and the Assistant Chief. No one mentioned the press conference, and the firestorm it created. I volunteered to organize a private meeting for city bar owners with the police, and they agreed this would help. To keep people safe in our city, we needed these two groups to communicate and work together.

A local newspaper called for the Commissioner to resign and to end her mayoral campaign, but she refused. On July 14, the Assistant Chief offered a public apology. That night, police arrested five people as dozens marched down Broadway to object to what he and the Commissioner said. As much as it seemed we made progress versus the pandemic, this conflict remained unfinished and now began to harm our city's reputation as a safe place to visit.

That's why I felt it was important at this moment to showcase that Saratoga was a destination where everyone was welcome to have fun. With July 4th coming up, the Saratoga Crew decided to invite the organizers of the Firecracker 4 road race to a Friday meeting. Even though no one had yet applied for a permit, everyone agreed to help host this event and we divided up the most important tasks to get this done.

Darryl and Ryan agreed to take the lead on the permit, while I found a race director and started to secure sponsors. The event website was set up and an email went out to past runners. Days before the run, we were still looking for water, snacks and bananas. It was a sprint to get this done, but again we made it happen.

Just over 2,000 people gathered on Broadway to run the 2021 Firecracker, Darryl and I were among them. People lined the streets to cheer for us. "It feels so good to run with other people again," a woman who stood near me at the starting line said. That day, the starter's pistol was the only gun that was fired and every news broadcast that night led with this positive story about Saratoga.

In 2020, Lisa and I "temporarily" delayed plans to travel to London. One year later in June of 2021, we were still banned from taking this trip. The COVID-19 situation there was now worse as they battled a new variant, called Delta. Even with rising vaccination rates, Delta became the most transmissible COVID the world had seen so far and this variant would reach Saratoga in early August.

Before Delta arrived, Lisa and I traveled again to the coast of Maine, and Katie and Ben met us there. On our first night, we enjoyed dinner indoors at a brewery with Jen and her husband. The next day, it was so cold we went to the movies in the afternoon, and gathered with thousands of people we didn't know to watch the fire-

works downtown. Every activity made it feel like we were returning to normal.

"We have a once in a lifetime opportunity to enjoy ourselves this summer," I suggested to the Saratoga Crew and the Chamber's staff. "I feel like local businesses will be busier than ever to make up for their losses. Others will simply be looking to finally have some fun too. No one will miss us until after Labor Day."

I joined a golf league and was on pace to run 500 miles for the year. Lisa and I planned our own vacation to Cape May in August. The Chamber's event schedule deliberately consisted of just one summer event at the Saratoga Race Course. The next two events would take place after Labor Day. This was the perfect set up for me to have a fun, relaxing summer, finally.

On July 16, the Saratoga Crew joined me at the Chamber's event at the Saratoga Race Course. Paid attendance that day topped 30,000 people. All summer, we'd see record breaking crowds as people came to Saratoga to gather with friends and family and to spend time at the track, SPAC, Live Nation, and the Casino.

I'M NOT READY FOR THIS...

As the six of us stood together at the rail in the warm sun, we were ready to enjoy the here and now. Locally, COVID-19 rates remained very low as vaccination rates increased. The six of us were ready to celebrate, so much so we even got dressed up with fancy hats, dresses and jackets. It was like the pandemic never happened, but that was not the reality.

The first week of August, Tracy, Craig, Jared, Joel, and Jason all had time-off from work and school. This was a rarity, so Tracy let the kids decide where their family would go on vacation. They wanted to spend time with Grammy Amy and decided to drive to Saratoga.

New York's current protocols said just three people at a time could visit with a resident. So on their first full day, Tracy, Joel and Jason visited Grammy Amy in the late morning. The plan was for Tracy, Craig and Jared to go the next day. Joel and Jared last saw Grammy in January of 2020. Jason and Craig had not seen her since June of 2019, more than two years ago.

"She was happy. She knew us, maybe not by name, but she knew she loved us. We had a wonderful visit," Tracy shared in a post. After this first visit, Lisa and I took them to the Saratoga Race Course, and I showed them how to bet on their phones. We had a great time together.

But just after 4:00 p.m., the Wesley sent us a text update, and the news was not good. An employee tested positive earlier that day, which meant they now had three employees with the virus. This triggered a new lockdown where only the two approved caregivers could visit. This meant Tracy and I could visit our mom, but Jared and Craig could not. Tracy was devastated, so I called the Wesley.

The only way Jared could visit was if he went right away. Tracy and Jared left the track immediately to go see Grammy Amy. As the elevator doors opened, they watched as my mom consoled a woman who was crying. She was in Nurse Amy mode.

"She had patient notes that she read to us. This was actually adorable," Tracy said. "It's obvious she can't read very well anymore. But she did get many of the medical terms right."

The next day, Tracy and I visited our mom together. She sat in her brown chair and held a small dog. Tracy and I wore masks. The three of us shared a large Wegmans chocolate chip cookie. She suggested this dog was dirty and needed a bath. Tracy and I looked at each other and laughed. We then tried to convince her that his fur was just two different colors, one was white and the other gray. She looked closely at him. "Maybe you're right," she said as she continued to pet him.

One day later, the visitation protocols changed again. Now I was required to put on a thin plastic blue hospital gown and a pair of latex gloves. A day later, a pair of goggles was added to the required PPE for visitors, and I was asked to visit in her room. The Wesley had to provide all of the PPE for their staff and visitors.

"How do you like my new wardrobe," I asked my mom. She just laughed as I spun around like a model. "I think I look good in blue plastic, don't you?"

Being here every day, I knew the staff members by name, and sometimes we chatted like friends or colleagues. Today, I saw the anguish on their faces. Their expressions clearly said, "I can't believe this is happening again." No one wanted to believe the pandemic was unfinished.

 Lisa Davis Shimkus
Aug 7, 2021

He'll probably not be happy that I posted this but I'm doing it anyway. I'm so tired and frustrated with people believing it against their rights to be "forced" to be vaccinated, or not believing the science behind the vaccine. This is what your personal choice and your thinking is doing to others. Because a staff member at my mother in law's nursing facility wasn't vaccinated and tested positive for COVID, this is how Todd had to dress to visit his mom. Our family has been fully vaccinated since we were first eligible to get the vaccine. None of us have been ill, we did it to keep ourselves, our loved ones, and the community at large healthy. But because of the selfishness, nearsightedness, and personal freedoms of others, this is how my husband gets to visit his mom. Stop complaining about your personal freedoms and give a care about something else besides yourself. Time to roll up your sleeve and get vaccinated! Help a guy out, who just wants to share a chocolate chip cookie with his mom.

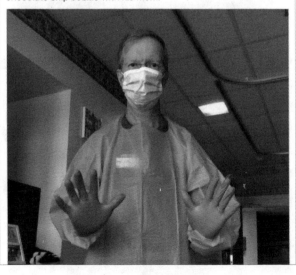

Wearing all of this PPE was uncomfortable. My glasses fogged up, and my hands were sweaty in the gloves. It was hot under the gown. As I grew more uncomfortable, I couldn't help but think about health care employees everywhere. They dressed like this all day for the better part of a year. How did they do it?

The next day, my mom was tired, a little agitated. No one knew why. She clearly didn't recognize me dressed like this. When I went to hold her hand, she looked at the glove and pulled her hand away. "That feels weird," she said. "Tell me about it," I responded. "Everything feels weird right now."

Lisa was incensed and just disappointed in this turn of events. "Because of the selfishness, nearsightedness, and personal freedoms of others, this is how my husband gets to visit his mom," she posted along with a photo of me. "Stop complaining about your personal freedoms and give a care about something else besides yourself. Time to roll up your sleeve and get vaccinated."

A year later, when Lisa and I were reunited with one of her brothers, I thanked him for the donations they made to the Wesley and the Alzheimer's Association in honor of my mom. Her brother responded, "I can't stop thinking about that photo of you dressed in the blue hospital gown. We felt so sorry for you and your mom."

But not everyone appreciated Lisa's post or believed in the vaccines. One of her nieces commented, "So much for being adults and showing others respect even if they disagree. Stop trying to push your views on everyone else, especially making something mandatory."

By early August of 2021, 80.6% of all eligible Saratoga residents had at least one vaccine dose. This meant there were more than 45,000 local residents who were unvaccinated. COVID-19 had not killed anyone in Saratoga since May 30, but this started to change as the Delta variant spread here. By year's end, nearly 100 more Saratoga residents would die from the virus, most were not fully vaccinated.

The job of leading New York's response to the Delta variant would not be Governor Cuomo's. On August 23, Cuomo resigned after New York's Attorney General released another scathing report. This time, she said he had violated federal and state workplace sexual harassment laws. She said she believed the 11 victims who bravely came forward despite his power and platform.

Darryl texted us: "Cuomo resigns. I can't believe it." Our responses ranged from, "Wowza," to "He is disgusting," to "What!!!!!" There was such a mix of emotions. Shock, surprise, anger, excitement and relief. Because I am convinced his policies traumatized my mom, I yelled, "Woooooo Hoooo," when I read Darryl's text so loud everyone in the Chamber office heard me.

Lieutenant Governor Kathy Hochul then became our new Governor. She had just been at SPAC to celebrate the opening of a new events center. She spoke glowingly about Saratoga, SPAC and the Track. Soon rather than cutting ribbons, she'd be the one to decide whether or not to impose a vaccine or mask mandate in New York, as it became increasingly obvious the virus was not done with us.

On August 26, my life changed dramatically too. While on vacation with Lisa in Cape May, I went body surfing and picked the wrong wave. It pounded me into the sand, my arms extended out in front of me, and I fractured the humerus bone in my right shoulder.

Being right handed, this wasn't funny and soon I found myself in pain, and more uncomfortable than ever before in my life. With my arm in a sling, I forced myself to learn how to do everything I could with just my left hand. Nothing was easy, and my frustration only grew as I learned how difficult it was to sleep with a broken shoulder.

A week later, Lisa was scheduled for knee surgery to repair a meniscus tear. She had been in pain for a long time, and I told her to keep the appointment. Publicly, we had some fun with our situation as we posed for a photo with me in a sling and her with crutches. The reality, however, was that we needed help.

"We have to figure out how not to be a burden on our kids," I often said to Lisa as she cared for her mom and dad, and now me with my mom. What we did to care for them was out of love, but it came with a price. There is nothing worse in life than watching someone you love die, often slowly over time. Your heart breaks for them as their health declines, and you feel helpless. You can do all the right and kind things and still feel like you could have done more.

But now Lisa and I had no choice as we had to ask for help from our kids. Unable to drive for two months, I gave Ben my car and we asked him to drive up every week. We joked that he was the executive director of the 203 Lake Avenue Rehabilitation Center, but what we faced was no joke. While I walked to work a lot and did the same to see my mom, I also learned to ask friends and co-workers for a ride when it rained or I didn't have time to walk.

> **Lisa Davis Shimkus** is with **Todd Shimkus**.
> Sep 2
>
> The Shimkus Rehab Center is now open! Todd added to my scheduled knee surgery last week when he broke his arm. Between the two of us, we make a functional human. 😜
>
> 👍😂😮 33   36 Comments

    Physically, Lisa was able to go to work a week later, as she didn't want to miss the first day of school with her new students. I too made it to work after Labor Day, and Deb installed a stand up desk in my office so I could type slowly with just my left hand. Lisa's knee and my shoulder would get better, but emotionally this trauma took a toll as we peered into our future and didn't like the never ending less-bad choices we likely will have to make as our overall health declines with age too.

FALL 2021

HEALTH CARE WORKERS had some difficult life choices to make now too. Just before leaving office, Cuomo imposed a vaccine mandate for all healthcare employees. He gave them until September 27 to comply, and said this action was needed to stop hospitalizations and deaths from the Delta variant. Soon after she took over as Governor, Kathy Hochul decided to keep this mandate in place, but not everyone complied.

"Hey Shimkus squared, I have some news to share," one of my mom's CNA's said to us. "I've decided to take a break from healthcare. I am sad to leave, but I need to try something else." When I asked, she told me she was hired to work at the Saratoga Casino. No doubt she had a difficult and stressful job, and she never mentioned the vaccine mandate. But as the deadline to get vaccinated passed, the Wesley lost five percent of its employees.

To deal with this, the Wesley transferred employees from other floors to 2 Victoria, and there were times when I saw senior staff members do what they could to help out. Eventually, they were forced to close entire units. The same thing happened at Saratoga Hospital. Both healthcare institutions lost staff because of this vaccine mandate during an already disruptive labor shortage.

Local hospitals banded together to encourage people to get vaccinated. "Let me be blunt," the chief medical officer of another local hospital said in a press release. "If you are not vaccinated, get the vaccine immediately. Your life, your loved one's lives, and those of your friends and neighbors depend on it."

To combat the Delta variant, the Federal government also authorized vaccine booster shots. Healthcare workers, older adults and those who lived in nursing homes were prioritized to get the shots first. I signed my mom up for a third dose, and she got the booster in late September. This was important because as this variant spread in the community, Wesley staff members who stayed on the job started to test positive again and had to quarantine.

Later in the Fall, the CDC would suggest that unvaccinated individuals were 11 times more likely to contract the Delta variant than those who were vaccinated. But there was a small percentage of cases where the virus broke through and a vaccinated person tested positive. Besides suggesting we were safer when vaccinated, there was little in the way of facts as to what caused these breakthroughs.

Was it the Delta variant? Did the vaccines become less effective over time? None of the vaccines provided 100 percent protection, so were these breakthroughs simply to be expected? Did these residents have comorbidities that made them more vulnerable? Without an-

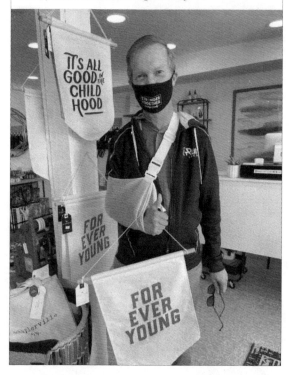

swers to these questions, those who opposed vaccine mandates pointed to the number of breakthrough cases as evidence that the vaccines didn't work.

Everyday when Tracy left to go anywhere, she traveled through the garage to leave her house. But her house was a model home in this development, and the garage was initially used as an office. When Tracy and Craig bought it, they remodeled this space to provide our mom with an in-law apartment.

Our mom had not lived there since June of 2019. But two years later, Tracy still had not changed a thing, until now. "I just painted mom's bedroom today," she texted me. "I moved stuff in to make it a craft, puzzle, sewing, office room for me. Thinking about her a lot. If you get a chance to FaceTime me or to use the portal, I'd love it."

With my injury, everything took me longer to do with just one functioning arm and hand, and I had to limit what I carried whenever I walked to see my mom. This meant I didn't bring my portal or iPad and I stopped doing virtual visits. I quickly responded and promised that I would do a virtual visit for her that weekend and more often in the weeks to come, not just for Tracy but everyone.

To my knowledge no matter how we interacted with my mom, we all did our best to protect my mom from all of the bad news in our world. Never once did we say the word COVID, pandemic, or virus to her. Since she entered the Wesley, I don't think I ever said the word Alzheimer's either. We didn't talk about her being in a nursing home, but she did love to talk and tell stories.

But now this simple pleasure became harder and harder. Once again, I didn't tell her or give her any indication at all that I had no idea what she was saying more and more often. When she couldn't find or didn't say the correct words, I simply listened and nodded my head. One day in October, I recorded our conversation.

"How's the dog?" I asked. She responded; "He's good. He gave a little late itch in the morning. He's diving for the kids. Frames and stuff. He knew I was back." She paused to laugh and I played along laughing too. "So that was nice. He could take anything that crushes this and put it in his tile. He was not a problem. He's not in that field yet. He'll go into it when someone else does. He looks like he's really tired. Looks like he's getting really big."

A couple weeks later, she just started to talk as soon as I sat down and I hit record on my cell phone. "So he's ready to bank it," her story began. She was animated, smiling, and looked right at me. I had no idea who he was. "So he banks it and he's standing in the back thinking he has to bank this today. He gets it. Puts a bake on it. Shuts the car. Gets out. As I'm walking around, I thought he's taking a bank now. Why's he doing that? So I don't know what's going on here. I'm thinking how can they do that? It's done and he's standing there. He's trying to say hello."

Whenever she spoke now, I leaned in real close and looked her in the eye. I wanted her to know I was listening, that her stories mattered. She sometimes randomly mentioned someone by name; Joanie, Betty, Tracy, Trisha, and even Todd. If she said my name, I'd ask her, "What did Todd do?" She'd laugh and continue with her story. I never once said but I'm Todd or Todd is here. Instead, this was a sign that somewhere in her brain she still knew me.

On October 16, Lisa and I took part in the local Walk to End Alzheimer's. Tracy and "Amy's Army" did the same thing in Virginia. These walks took place across the country and every walker is invited to choose a flower to carry. There is no getting through the opening ceremony at each walk without some tears.

The yellow flowers are for caregivers like Tracy, Trisha and me, and the blue flower is for those with Alzheimer's. The flower we want is white, as this will be given to the first person cured of this miserable disease. The Alzheimer's Association gives a purple flower to those who have lost someone to this disease. Someday, all of us in Amy's Army will carry a purple flower. This thought made me cry at this year's walk as I could see that day was approaching.

Before the walk in Virginia, the Alzheimer's Association asked Tracy if she was willing to share her story with a local newspaper, and she said yes. "I have felt helpless throughout COVID to assist my mom," Tracy said to the reporter. "There is little I can do for her now, but I can walk and raise money and hope that one day we end Alzheimers."

According to the National Institute of Health, Alzheimer's disease is the sixth leading cause of death in the US. It is named after Dr. Alois Alzheimer's. In the early 1900's, Dr. Alzheimer's treated a woman who

died of an unusual mental illness. After she died, he examined her brain and found several "plaques and tangles." We now know more about this plaque buildup, and that it progresses starting with an early stage of Alzheimer's, and then a mild, moderate and severe one.

"People with severe Alzeimer's cannot communicate and are completely dependent on others for their care," the NIH advised. "Near the end of life, the person may be in bed most or all of the time as the body shuts down." This was where my mom was headed, and there was not a thing we could do about it.

As Amy's Army walked, my mom started to struggle to do the same. She limped more and more now, and favored her left leg. Her once brisk pace reduced to a slow shuffle with her walker. No more Nurse Amy doing rounds or going for walks with her dog and me in the corridors. We couldn't tell if it was the hip she broke, the knee she had replaced, or her foot that was swollen. "All tests were negative. They found nothing," I texted Tracy.

Her physical and mental decline changed the focus of my visits. No longer built around a walk or a conversation, my goal was much simpler - to make a connection and to be sure she knew she was loved. She smiled whenever I walked in and twirled around. If I gave her a big hug, she sometimes said, "I like that." Just make sure she was happy for at least one moment each day was my plan and the best I could offer.

On Halloween, this was an easy goal to accomplish. Lisa came with me for this visit, and I brought my horse costume. Dressed in this costume, everyone laughed as I entered the front door of the facility. As soon as I got off the elevator, everyone in the living room turned to see me. The staff laughed out loud and came out to see who it was dressed like this with my face hidden by the costume and my mask.

Slowly I walked toward my mom, she raised her right hand, and I lowered my horse head so she could pet it. I did the same with Judy and the other residents who sat near her. When I moved away from them, I stopped and shook my tail to get others to smile. This was a moment of pure joy that I will never forget, and it was proof that even in the worst of times that laughter and being together are vital to our well-being.

By early November, I wished there was some way for me to make everyone laugh. People everywhere struggled with the emotional and mental impacts of the continued uncertainty and division. In Saratoga and elsewhere, people fought over mask and vaccination mandates, and no one knew when this third wave might subside or if there might be more.

On Instagram, a friend posted: "Raise your hand if you agree with any of the following: I'm tired. I'm exhausted. I'm struggling. I've reached my breaking point. I'm actually past my breaking point. Sometimes I feel hopeless."

On Twitter, another friend posted. "Anyone else ever get really sad and lonely because you have friends all over the country that you haven't seen in 2 years but you can't even attempt to make plans to see them any time soon until the world stops ending."

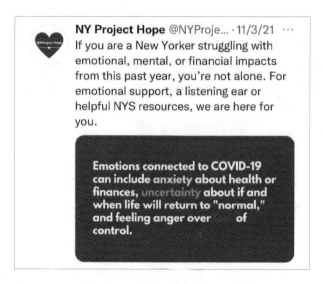

With testing positivity on the rise again, Deb Zeman feared that it was not safe for us to work together at the Chamber. Several employees had relatives and close friends who contracted the virus or were home sick. She implored me to establish and share stronger protocols, and I reminded everyone that if they felt sick in any way to stay home and get tested.

"OMG, I cannot do this job anymore," Lisa texted me. Every day, she left the house by 6:45 am and she was rarely home by 6:00 p.m. On Sundays, she spent at least 8 hours getting prepared for the next week. There was a far greater diversity of student capabilities in this year's class, and this required more differentiated instruction. Instead of one lesson plan, she created at least a half dozen, for math, reading, writing and science.

Meanwhile, Ben now worked three part-time jobs, two retail and one at a restaurant in Brooklyn. "That was me making exactly $1 in tips yesterday," Ben texted along with a note from his employer after a shift at the restaurant. After he left that job, he was offered a contract to perform again on a cruise ship. But their COVID protocols confined employees to the ship for at least eight months. This didn't feel safe or right, so he said no.

I did not get a free pass from the trauma, even though I did everything I could so it looked that way. My shoulder was still uncomfortable and the physical therapy was painful; it was now obvious that it would take months for me to regain even a little range of motion. Simultaneously, I watched the things that my mom once told me defined her quality of life slowly disappear. Life for me was in slow motion, still reliant on my left hand and powerless to change the downward trajectory of my mom's health.

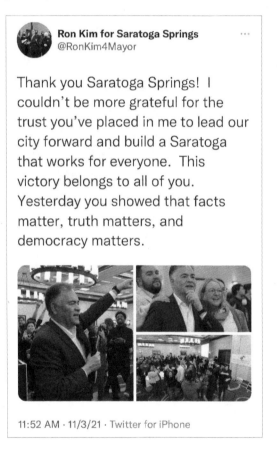

COVID-19 didn't just disrupt our lives and economy, there was significant political fallout too. In 2020, President Trump was defeated and the Democrats gained control of the Senate and the House. After being called a pandemic hero by many, Cuomo resigned in disgrace in 2021 and was replaced by his Lieutenant Governor. The Saratoga County Board of Supervisors let go of a 33 year employee to hire a new county administrator in early 2021 as the elected leadership on the Board changed as well.

In early November, city residents elected four new leaders, with only the Commissioner of Public Works winning re-election. The Mayor, the Commissioners of Finance and Accounts didn't lose, but rather decided not to run as they took their place in what was now nationally called: "The Great Resignation." Commissioner Dalton ran for Mayor and came in a distant third. Three of the five newly elected Commissioners had never served in elected office before.

Our new Mayor, Ron Kim, was the first Asian-American elected a mayor of a city in New York State. The city's new Finance Commissioner, Minita Sangavi, was the first openly gay Commissioner. The Saratoga Crew met together with each of the newly elected leaders before they took office. We wanted to work with them to make it easier to host events, resolve the differences between the police department and protesters, and to make expanded outdoor dining permanent.

WINTER 2021

JUST AFTER THANKSGIVING, a new variant, referred to as Omicron, was detected first in South Africa. On December 2, lab testing confirmed New York's first positive case of this variant. Even though more than 90 percent of all adult New Yorkers now had at least one dose of the vaccine, this variant spread even faster than Delta.

"Get vaccinated, get your booster, get tested, and wear a mask," Governor Hochul tweeted. "You are ten times more likely to be hospitalized with COVID-19 if you're not vaccinated," she warned. One week later as the positivity rate rose, she imposed a new mask mandate that would start December 13.

The Chamber immediately emailed news of this mandate, and we included a new poster for recipients to print and display again with the Stronger Together and Chamber logos. This poster said: "Masks Required in all indoor public places per New York State Governor Kathy Hochul." Not everyone was happy.

"Very disappointed to see the Chamber assisting in pushing the Governor's irrational mandate when they should be fighting it," a local business owner replied. Two days later, Saratoga County's leaders told the Governor that they lacked the resources to enforce this mandate. Instead, they declared their priority was to respond to the local surge in demand for tests and vaccinations.

With no clear way for the state to enforce this mandate, business owners had to again decide whether or not to ask their employees to police their customers. They also knew that some customers and employees would not enter a business that required masks, while others would refuse to patronize or work at businesses that didn't require masks. It was a no-win situation.

The spread of Omicron around the world resulted in significant and sometimes unexplainable supply shortages. Car dealers couldn't get cars, largely because of a shortage of computer chips. A local pet store reported a shortage of superworms and crickets. The price of chicken wings tripled. I couldn't find Rice Krispies for weeks. The randomness of these shortages and price fluctuations was unbelievable. We would soon see a significant rise in inflation and then interest rates as the government sought to cool down the economy.

This is why no one questioned the Chamber's plans for a second annual Save Our Locals campaign. This time, we incentivized people to shop local by purchasing $6,000 in gift cards from local businesses.

Anyone who sent us a receipt that showed they purchased a good or service valued at more than $20.21 at a locally owned business was eligible to win. The same was true for anyone who made a donation to a local nonprofit. More than 2,000 people participated, and they spent and donated nearly $200,000 to save our locals.

Healthcare workers also continued to deal with a range of emotions. "Our team has been fighting the pandemic for nearly two years, and they are exhausted," the Hospital's chief nursing officer shared with me. "Lately, some are discouraged because much of the recent sickness and death could have been prevented. Yet, as I see firsthand every day, they remain committed to taking care of each patient with skill and compassion."

To support them, I reached out to the original organizers of the 2020 Front Line Appreciation Group or FLAG Saratoga. The Chamber offered them $5,000 in seed funds to restart this program. Everyone said yes, and the first deliveries of wellness products and grab and go snacks reached hundreds of local healthcare workers after the New Year. Each gift basket also included heartfelt thank you notes designed and written by local school children.

On December 9, Trisha visited our mom and delivered her a gift, a new photo of Tyler. She told me the visit was "very good." Later that day, she did a post and her final comment spoke to the stress we all felt after our visits these days, "Please don't forget me, mommy."

My mom was increasingly uncomfortable, and when she was she became combative. One of the CNA's showed me a scratch on her wrist from one of their battles. I now often found my mom asleep, and she spent a lot more time alone in her room. Her nurse called regularly to let me know my mom fell out of a chair, her bed, or was found on the floor. She no longer had the strength to get up to walk, but she'd forget and try anyway.

We needed to do something special to lift her spirits, and Tracy had an idea. "So we were thinking we'd drive to Saratoga on Christmas Day. We will bring Ribbie. Maybe we can bring him to go see mom, but what do you think?" I said yes immediately. This reunion could only help her, even if for just a moment.

When Tracy arrived for this visit on Christmas Day, she found our mom in the cafeteria. Her head was slumped and she was asleep in a chair in what looked like a very uncomfortable position. When Tracy woke her up, she didn't want to talk, so Tracy just wheeled her into her room.

"Look who's here," Tracy said to our mom as Ribbie came into the room after her. My mom saw him and held out her arms to pick him up. "Oh there's the boy, look at him. Look at him," my mom exclaimed. She spoke in complete sentences and used the right words. "Come here baby. I haven't seen you in so long," my mom added. Ribbie recognized her too, and he never left her side.

As I watched the video of this reunion later, my mom came alive and her Alzheimer's disappeared. She became the dog lady one last time. It had been more than 2 years since they were together, but it was Christmas Day and this was our gift to her.

Tracy Shimkus Cheifetz
Dec 25, 2021

Merry Christmas!! We had a very nice day. Drove to New York and went to visit my Mom...brought RBI in to see her - first time she has seen him since 9/2019. We had a nice visit but it was so hard to leave her, especially on Christmas! Then we got to see my brother, his wife, and my niece and nephew. This trip has been so good for my soul. We are not meant to be away from our loved ones for so long!! Quick visit with my Mom tomorrow then we are heading home.

Tracy, Craig, Joel, Jason and Ribbie came to our house after this visit. Katie and Ben were here too. Last year, our families celebrated virtually and played online games. Today, we played "Cards Against Humanity" and I can say that I've never seen Craig laugh so hard. We all did as we sat in our living room near the fireplace. We were all vaccinated and boosted, but I still kept a window open to circulate some air just to be safe.

Not everyone was as lucky. My cousin Jen's son, Ryan, came home from college, and tested positive for COVID. He was asymptomatic, but he was required to quarantine. Suddenly, it was unsafe for Joanie and Betty to spend time with them on Christmas Day. "You know what else this tells me, our kids' mental health is not good," Jen texted me. "Poor Ryan is scared to come out of his room because he doesn't want to get us sick. Please 2022 be kind."

JANUARY 2022

THERE WERE AGAIN no fireworks in Saratoga, and no First Night Celebration of any kind. It still was not safe for people to gather like we once did. This was the third New Year in a row when the virus surged.

From a small cluster of cases in Wuhan, China, on January 1, 2020, until New Year's Day, 2022, the virus had killed at least six million people. The number of Americans killed topped 800,000, and this number continued to climb as Omicron was now the fastest spreading variant so far with both vaccinated and unvaccinated people getting sick.

One year ago, we thought the worst was over and that the discovery of vaccines would stop the spread of COVID-19. Now, there was little information to boost our confidence and our faith in what the experts told us waned. This didn't stop them from suggesting that it looked like the virus was now less lethal, particularly for those who were vaccinated.

The spread of Omicron in New York State was dramatic, and Saratoga exemplified this disturbing trend. During the past two years, just under 30,000 residents tested positive for the virus. But in the first month of 2022, another 14,000 residents would test positive.

To keep nursing home residents safe, Governor Hochul decided to impose new restrictions. Most alarming, she required visitors to present a negative test to enter these facilities. Perhaps this was reasonable, but the availability of tests was still limited and I feared this might keep me and others from being able to visit our loved ones.

For instance, the Wesley averaged 100 visitors per day, most were elderly. Some visited every day, yet no one had a plan to ensure tests were available. "I feel bad for nursing homes," I tweeted. "Testing supplies are scarce and there is a cost to get tested. Tomorrow, there will be residents who will be alone, isolated. For how long?"

Friends who saw my post rescued me, as dozens of tests were dropped off at my home. "We know how much seeing your mom every day means," a friend said in a note attached to the kits they left in a gift bag on our porch. Lisa told me that a teacher at her school had a husband who was in a nursing home. She visited him every day and couldn't get any test kits. I shared some of mine with her, and as my personal supply increased significantly, I did the same with other family members I saw on 2 Victoria.

Todd Shimkus @ToddShimk... · 1/8/22

Nurse Amy had skeptical look today. She can't say it so I will. Possible @HealthNYGov testing requirement for nursing home visits seems impractical w/ demand for tests outstripping supplies. Plus omicron replicates faster in throat & mouth, not nose. Pls don't separate us again!

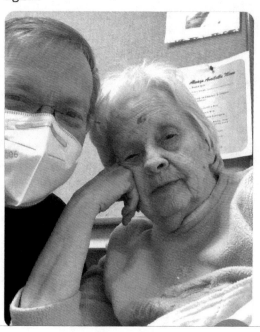

One of my goals for 2022 was to change my mom's personal care plan. "I talked with the Wesley team about palliative care," I texted Tracy. "My concern is that she's in pain almost every day and has essentially lost the ability to walk on her own. I want to be sure she is safe, comfortable and pain free." Tracy agreed with this new focus.

Once I signed the paperwork, the nurses started to use a patch to deliver pain medication more often. If she was uncomfortable when she needed to move, the staff now used a wheelchair. Routine health monitoring activities that might upset her were canceled, and all dietary restrictions were lifted. "Let her eat all the chocolate chip cookies she wants," I said to her team as everyone laughed.

The first day after this change, she was asleep in a reclining chair in the living room, and I could not wake her up. The second day, I was told she didn't eat or drink that much. The third day, she ate breakfast but did not want to be moved. On the fourth day, she was awake and alert enough or so I thought for me to FaceTime with Tracy and Trisha. But sitting in the living room, she was confused, distracted, and lost interest quickly.

After this call, I tried to get her to sing happy birthday to Tracy. I sang the song myself the first time to remind her of the words. She told me she was ready, and I turned on the camera. "Okay Tracy, habba dury carry," she said. I asked her to try one more time and she said the same exact thing. This time at the end, she gave me a look that said, what more do you want from me? It was such a cute look that I decided to send Tracy the video anyways.

The Omicron surge continued, and this made it hard for Discover Saratoga to move forward with Chowderfest in early February. State and city leaders didn't feel comfortable approving the permit to host this mass gathering, knowing it attracted tens of thousands of people to the downtown. At our second Friday meetup in January, Darryl shared with us that this event was rescheduled for March 26.

Knowing how important this event was to local restaurants in need of cash to pay their bills, I offered to move the Chamber's Restaurant Week from March to February. This demonstrated continued collaboration among our organizations, and gave people a way to support local restaurants in February and March.

The city's new leaders stepped in to help too, as they cut the Chowderfest bill for police, fire, and public works services in half. Likewise, the Chamber's staff secured sponsors for our February restaurant week, which allowed us to make it free for restaurants to participate. The Saratoga Crew dined out one night together for restaurant week, and we traveled together to multiple locations during Chowderfest.

At his first State of the City address, Mayor Kim recognized Ryan, Darryl, Deann, Shelby, Sam and me by name for the work we did to save Saratoga's local businesses. We continued to meet, as friends and collaborators, and often now our city's elected leaders joined us. With our support, the city extended the use of public spaces for outdoor patios for two years and made it easier and less expensive to host events downtown. They also investigated the death of Darryl Mount and established a police review commission, and this brought an end to the protests which made everyone feel better.

On a visit in February, my mom was awake, alert, and happy. "I like it when you are here," she told me. I smiled and gave her a big hug. "I like that too," she added as she kissed my forehead. I told her that I loved her, and she responded, "I love you too."

Unfortunately, this visit was the exception, as most didn't go anywhere near as well. She cried whenever the staff stood her up to get her into or out of the wheelchair or her bed. Trips to the bathroom were the worst. Most times, the CNA's closed the door and suggested I wait outside her room. But even then, I could hear her as she yelled, "No, no, no. It hurts. You're hurting me. Stop. Stop."

A couple of times these cries went on so long that I went in to see if my voice or presence might calm her down. This was never how I expected to see my mom. My being there made no difference, as I couldn't take away the pain or the anxiety she felt. When the CNA's were done, she stopped crying and sat in the wheelchair exhausted from the fight. It was then my job to get her to forget what just transpired.

One day, Amanda, one of her CNA's sat down with the two of us. Amanda looked at me and said, "Todd, you really are a good son. I just want you to know that it's going to get a lot harder. She's not going to recognize you and she will stop talking. You may not recognize her. It will be very tough, and I just want you to be prepared."

A few days later on February 9 as my visit ended, I wheeled my mom to the cafeteria for lunch. The activities director was coloring with the residents. Valentine's Day was near and she gave everyone a coloring page that said "Love, Me." I gave one of these pages where these words had been pre-colored to my mom and told her to hold it up and smile. Her smile was genuine, and at that moment she felt good and was happy. This was the last photo I ever took of my mom.

My mom was not the only one in our family that struggled with end of life challenges. Sammi, our eleven pound Morkie, a Maltese and Yorkshire mix, was also diagnosed with early dementia and kidney failure. Besides visiting my mom every day, I now went home twice a day to check in on him too.

Lisa rescued Sammi when he was two years old from a local shelter thirteen years ago, in 2009, soon after her dad passed. The two of them bonded immediately. I often described Sammi as a cat that barked. He loved to snuggle, refused to wear a collar, hated car rides and going for walks. But he was perfect for us, and until recently never required much more than some attention, grain-free food and to be let out into a fenced yard where he could do his business and chase the squirrels or the rabbits.

Like I did with my mom, I consulted with Sammi's doctor and she did a bunch of tests. One day, she asked me; "Is there any joy left in his life?" I thought this was such a great question to ask not just for Sammi but for my mom. I told her Sammi had moments of joy, particularly in the mornings when he followed Lisa around the house, and I watched his tail wag while he looked for food or attention. The same was true at night when she came home.

Each of these moments of joy now lasted no more than ten minutes. Oftentimes when I came home to check on him, I'd find him under the bed as he whimpered. It was impossible to know if he was in pain or just frustrated because he could no longer jump up onto the bed to be where he wanted to sleep.

On February 22, the Veterinarian came to our home to put Sammi to rest while both Lisa and I held him. He passed peacefully and the care shown to us was non-judgemental and comforting. She never said we did the right thing but it was implied. That night, I was not just sad because we lost Sammi, but I was angry, furious really.

"We're allowed to treat our pets better at the end of their lives than we can the people we love," I said to Lisa and anyone who listened days later. My little buddy, as I called Sammi, died in a loving and humane way. Meanwhile there was so little joy in my mom's life as she suffered, asleep most of the time, and totally reliant on others for every basic need. "Why can't we help my mom to die peacefully too?" I asked over and over.

In late February, as I sat in the living room on 2 Victoria, my mom asleep in a recliner, the nurse suggested I consider hospice care. "We love your mom and she wouldn't have to leave this floor," she told me. "Instead, she'd get more support, from a hospice nurse, and you could talk to them as well." I said yes, as I knew it was time.

That weekend, I reached out to my sisters and Joanie to suggest they visit right away. Trisha drove to Saratoga on February 28; Tracy visited March 2 and 3rd; Joanie and Betty came on March 4; and Katie came out that weekend. My mom was awake to visit with everyone except for Katie; the other visits likely drained her limited energy.

When I visited again by myself on Monday, March 7, my mom was confined to her bed. The staff now dressed her in a hospital gown so they didn't have to change her clothes or make her stand up in the bathroom. With hospice, she could receive morphine, but they struggled at first to figure out the right schedule and dosage.

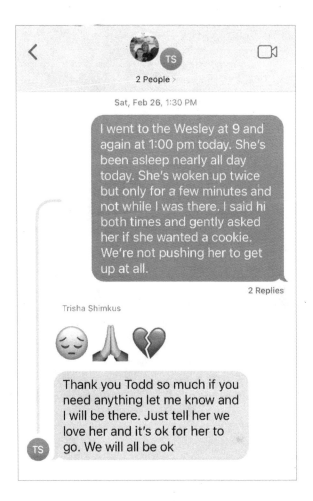

Amanda was right, as these visits were the hardest. My mom couldn't talk and cried when she was awake. I was powerless to help her. The best I could do was to make sure her dogs were within her reach, and I played music while holding her hand. I just felt bad for her. This was not fair, nor was it how she wanted her life to end.

MARCH 13, 2022

THE TWO YEAR ANNIVERSARY of the start of the pandemic was upon us. No one celebrated. Nor were we free of the virus. According to the New York Times, a whopping 500 million people across the world had tested positive, and millions more would get sick in the days, weeks and months to come.

Americans 65 years old or older made up three fourths of the nearly 1 million deaths we had in our nation, and as many as 140,000 of those who died were nursing home residents. In spite of having perhaps the most significant and prolonged shutdown, restrictions, protocols, and mandates, New York State recorded the most deaths.

We sacrificed so much in New York, and for what? On a conference call with Chamber executives from around the country, I mentioned that I still wore a mask and had to be tested every three days to visit my mom. A peer from a chamber in Florida chuckled and said, "Todd, I haven't worn a mask in a year, nor do I know where to find one."

Locally in Saratoga, this first Omicron surge subsided for now, and even during its height the number of hospitalizations and deaths was far

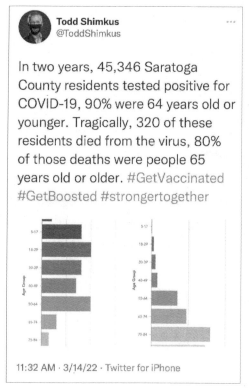

less than the other surges. The experts suggested this was because of the vaccines, but there was no such option to save my mom's life from Alzheimer's.

On March 13, the morphine began to work and my mom finally stopped crying. Now as both her mind and body failed her, she stopped eating. Craig advised that most people pass away within eleven days after they stop eating, so I started to count down the days as I wanted her suffering to end.

My visits were longer now, as she was confined to her bed and I didn't want her to be alone. Some days, I worked from her bedside, just in case she woke up. Whenever I was in her room, I broke state protocols and took off my mask. If she opened her eyes, I wanted to be sure she saw my entire face and had the best chance possible to know that it was me by her side. As each day passed, the hospice nurses and the CNA's said, "she's one tough cookie." I would respond, "make that a chocolate chip cookie."

In spite of everything Alzheimer's and COVID did to my mom, she didn't want to die.

On March 19, I was given a special gift. Amanda came into the room and stood directly behind me as I sat in a chair next to my mom's bed. My mom's eyes were slightly open and she was awake, but she was unable to speak.

"Hey Todd, did you see that?," Amanda asked me as I turned around to look at her. "I can read lips. It's a secret power of mine. Your mom just whispered that she loves you. Turn around and tell her you love her too."

I did as she advised, and immediately thought that this was the kindest thing anyone had ever done for me. That night, I sent a note to the Wesley's CEO and shared this story. He asked if I wanted to nominate Amanda for one of the organization's "compassion awards," and I said yes. Several weeks later, Amanda received the award and reached out to thank me. Nominating her for this award was the least I could do.

On March 23, the hospice nurse called and said that my mom's breathing indicated this might be the day. Trisha was already on her way to Saratoga for a visit, so I went to sit with my mom right away. When Trisha arrived, I somehow managed to leave for a few hours and facilitated two meetings, and returned to her room at 2:30 p.m.

Trisha was on one side of her bed, and I was on the other. Three of my mom's stuffed animal dogs were with her, one under each arm and the other rested comfortably on her chest. She was covered by the Ribbie blanket Tracy made for her. She couldn't walk with her dog, but he was right there until the end just like us.

The room was very quiet, and neither of us said a thing. My mom's breathing slowed and there were moments where we thought it stopped, but then she rallied one more time. She soon took her last breath, a courageous decade long battle with Alzheimer's and a lifetime of caring for others over.

Even though I told her it was okay to go, I was not ready to lose my mom. When I leaned in to tell her I loved her one last time, I couldn't finish the sentence and sobbed uncontrollably with my head buried in her pillow. It was a good thing that Trisha was there as she walked over to help me stand up and gave me a hug. "Mom waited for you to come back," she said as I tried to regain my composure.

From December 26, 2019, until March 23, 2022, I visited my mom nearly 450 times. It would have been over 800 visits were it not for COVID and the one-year long isolation imposed by our state government. If I remember correctly, every member of the staff came to see me and Trisha to make sure we were okay as word spread about my mom's death. The next day, Tracy called what I did to care and advocate for our mom a "crusade."

One of my favorite quotes is: "The world is run by those who show up." I don't remember who first said this to me, but I share this phrase with people all the time. When it came to caring for my mom and my community, I showed up these last two years whenever and wherever I was needed and allowed.

> MAR 25, 7:55 PM
>
> Hey buddy. I had the day off when your mom passed. I'm so sorry for your loss. I enjoyed taking care of your mom and you are my favorite and nicest family member of a resident I've ever met. Thank you for always being kind to myself and my other staff members. And I'll never forget what you did for Emily and I at comic con. I hope to see you around some day.

My mom had passed, but the crusade was not over. In lieu of flowers, I asked those who wanted to honor my mom to drop off stuffed animals on my porch. For the next two weeks when I arrived home, I went out to the porch every day and found more and more dogs, cats, rabbits, bears, and other stuffed animals in all shapes and sizes. Pretty soon, we filled 8 boxes with stuffed animals, and it brought me great joy to deliver them not just to the Wesley, but to other organizations who cared for individuals that would enjoy receiving one.

Likewise, Tracy set up an Amy's Army team to walk in her local Walk to End Alzheimer's, and she invited her friends to make a donation. The fundraising goal was increased three times as donations poured in from friends and family. Trisha, Tracy and I also worked together to plan a family-only celebration of life for our mom.

On April 16, forty members of our extended family gathered for this celebration at a local restaurant in Massachusetts that Trisha selected. Joanie and Betty ordered the flowers; Tracy prepared a slide show with hundreds of photos; Katie, Ben and Jason performed a song; and Tracy and Trisha each delivered a eulogy. My mom would have loved all of this.

Normally, I would have done more to lead and organize this event, but the only thing I wanted to do was to go for a walk with Ribbie. I just thought my mom would like this more than any of the usual funeral traditions. So I was patient, and did my best to engage with everyone and to thank them for coming. When the extended family left, rain fell outside and suddenly my planned walk on a local trail was out of the question.

Thankfully as we drove to the celebration that morning, I saw an ice cream stand near the restaurant. It was one that my mom took us to when we lived in Holden. So I suggested we go there, and as we arrived I realized that just across the parking lot was a covered patio with lots of seating. After we got our ice cream, we walked to this patio as a family with Ribbie leading the way. He was now our therapy dog.

SPRING 2022

Two days after my mom's celebration of life was April 18, and my 55th birthday. I was in Boston with Lisa, Katie, and Ben. This trip was a chance to move from celebrating my mom's life to enjoying my own. I hoped the time our family spent together here would create memories the four of us would cherish for the rest of our lives.

That morning, Tracy sent me a copy of the video of my mom singing Happy Birthday to me - - the one she filmed virtually in April of 2020. On that day, my mom sang this song perfectly, and when she finished she smiled joyously. Like the blanket she sent Trisha, this was a special gift for me. For the rest of my life, I will be able to play this video to see and hear my mom when she was happy as she did something she loved to do.

On April 20, my mom would have turned 78. Her birthday, like the day she died, will now be among the days that remind us of her absence and our loss. "Miss you mom. So very much. Happy birthday my angel, my best friend, my mom," Trisha wrote on Facebook. Soon we faced our

Don't want to start your day off sad, but birthdays were important to her and she'd want to wish you a happy birthday!! And hopefully the end of this makes you laugh.

first Mother's Day without her, and I wore my Amy's Army shirt as I gathered with a thousand runners for the first in-person Mother Lovin 5K since 2019. I ran much faster than I expected which I took as a sign that she was still a spectator watching me compete.

My mom was gone from this earth, but the virus was not. In the next month, more people I knew tested positive than at any time in the past two years. This included Lisa and Ben, as well as five members of the Chamber's staff. Everyone reported slightly different symptoms, but they didn't last more than a couple of days, and thankfully no one I knew was hospitalized or died.

For the rest of 2022, I monitored the 7-day average number of deaths on the NY Times homepage, as the rate of deaths continued to range from 300 to 500 every seven days. Governor Hochul extended the State of Emergency until the summer was over, but no new protocols were enacted and most of us went about our lives as if the virus never existed. The pandemic was not done with us, but we were done with it.

I thought about my mom every day as I looked at my daily schedule and "visit mom" was no longer listed as an imperative action. In many respects, the loss of my mom, Sammi, and the end of the pandemic offered Lisa and me tremendous freedom and flexibility. We had the time and resources to go wherever we wanted, but it was not that easy.

During the crisis, we focused on survival, and getting through each day. We never felt confident enough to make any long term plans. The near constant changes that came with each new variant or surge, and the resulting protocols meant that we lived in the moment just like my mom. With such uncertainty, there was an adrenaline rush to everything I did, but this vanished as soon as my mom and Saratoga no longer needed to be saved.

Turns out, writing this book became what I did in my free time as I worked nights and weekends on it for months. Every time I edited a section felt like a chance to spend time with my mom again. Alzheimer's and the pandemic did their best to separate us, but the more I relived this experience the more I felt like she and I were closer these past two years than ever before.

Creating one positive moment for her everyday made both of us happy. Alzheimer's is a miserable disease but I will never use that word to describe our time together. So to those who find themselves on a caregiving journey, I want you to know that I have no regrets placing my mom at the Wesley. That's because as the heroes that worked there cared for her, I was given the freedom to focus on making her smile.

Just like me, Lisa would soon have more free time too. She was now done spending six days a week, ten hours a day, to be a super good teacher. So when this school year ended, she "retired" and donated the vast majority of the books, furniture, and classroom supplies she amassed to other teachers, as she searched for a new calling.

Ben stopped auditioning all together to pursue a Master's Degree in Journalism. He wanted to use his voice to advocate for victims. Katie wanted a change too, as she did not like to work from 11:30 am to 8 pm to match her west coast based co-workers. After she completed an online certificate program in linguistics, she hoped to return to school to get a PhD and maybe even study the language patterns of those with Alzheimer's.

"So what are you doing today?" my mom often asked me. Some days, I told her I was writing a book. "What is it about?" she asked on her better days. To which I replied, "It's about you." Then she'd laugh and give me a look that said, "Who would write a book about me?" Well I did because I believe her story needed to be told and mine too.

There were approximately 100,000 nursing home residents in New York State when the pandemic struck and the lockdown began. The 15,000 who died and their families suffered for sure, but so did the survivors who spent more than a year isolated from loved ones. After the lockdown ended, a Wesley employee shared with me, "I cried every night when I got home. We have no idea how much damage was done to those poor people."

This forced and prolonged isolation was cruel, unfair, and must never happen again. In fact, I hope that when we face our next public health crisis that we will value mental health just as much as physical health, because I don't think you can have one without the other.

But this book is also my narrative of hope as I am confident that all of us who survived the range of threats and disruptions this pandemic wrought are more resilient today than we were on March 13,

2020. We all learned to be more resilient and as a result we are better prepared for whatever life throws at us next. Resilience is our new super power, and if we realize this then we can thrive no matter what we do next.

Of course, the key to being resilient is to have the love and support of others. In my story, I cannot possibly understate how vital it was for me to be supported by my family, the Chamber staff, and the Saratoga Crew. Everything we did was a team effort, a collaboration, and the moments we spent together on the porch, in the city center, in the office, and in our community are memories I will cherish forever. We really were Stronger Together, and we always will be!

With Kindness,
Todd Shimkus

ACKNOWLEDGEMENTS

When the pandemic began, I still believe the best thing that I did was to surround myself with the people I loved. Lisa, Katie, and Ben were with me in Saratoga, and their presence every day made a difference and allowed me to do whatever I needed to do to help my mom and my community.

I stayed in close contact with Tracy, Trisha, Craig, Joanie, Betty and Jen as we worked together to support my mom and to check in on one another. Each of them at varying times came to her rescue and mine.

The Chamber staff - - Deb, Richie, Sara, Andrea, Liz, Denise, Annamaria, Kathleen, Maddie, and Devin - - were always available to help and did most of the actual work so the Chamber could save our community. The Saratoga Crew - - Darryl, Deann, Ryan, Samantha, and Shelby - - were incredible partners, collaborators, and became forever friends.

The Chamber's Board of Directors, particularly Kevin Hedley and Skip Carlson, provided incredible leadership as we faced this threat to our economy and organization. Angelo Calbone and his COVID-19 team at Saratoga Hospital were always available as we sought to provide our local community with the best advice. Led by Jack Lawler and Spencer Hellwig, the Saratoga Reopening Committee became a valuable partner in our effort to share the best advice we could to keep people safe and businesses open.

No doubt a lot of people in the community asked for my help and advice. But I do believe that an equal number reached out to find out what they could do to help me and to save our community. Now every week, I get thanked by people I don't even know, and I want everyone who offered such support and kindness to know this inspires me to want to do more.

When I decided to try to write this book, Katie told me to "just start writing and don't stop," For Christmas that year, she registered me for a writing class via GrubStreet which is how I met Katie Bannon. That class and the follow up advice from both Katie's helped me become a better writer, and taught me how to tie the various storylines together into this memoir.

Lisa and Tracy read very early drafts when the story was not even finished. Katie did line-edits for free on at least three different versions. No way I finish this project without their help, suggestions, and support. I knew this book was ready to be published when Lisa read the latest draft and couldn't put it down, and Tracy told me that she thought she had visited with our mom simply by reading it.

Chris Morrow, Ray O'Conor, and Greg Veitch helped me understand my options to get this book published. Nick and Barbara Caimano provided advice that helped me to tell a less political and more accurate account of what happened. I wish that I had consulted with The Troy Book Makers earlier in the process as their advice on how to actually include the images of text messages, photos, and social posts was huge.

The real heroes in this story are the people who worked at the Wesley, in particular on 2 Victoria. My family will forever be in their debt for the care and compassion they showed my mom, especially when we were not allowed to be there to help. The same goes for the staff at Saratoga Hospital who cared for her after she broke her hip, and to my friends in the Alzheimer's community who taught me how to care for and communicate with my mom.

In the Fall of 2022, Amy's Army took part in three walks to end Alzheimer's, and we raised nearly $17,000. To everyone who donated money to this cause or a stuffed animal to help us remember my mom, thank you. I want to thank everyone who buys this book as the net proceeds will help us to raise even more money for Amy's Army and the effort to end Alzheimer's and to help those who care for those with the disease.

In this book, the statistics I shared detailing the spread and impact of the virus and the effort to get people vaccinated were sourced from the World Health Organization, the CDC, the New York Times, the Saratoga County COVID-19 database, and the Times Union. I also made extensive use of social media which allowed me to gather additional information and to quote so many people, from my sisters, to Governor Cuomo, etc.

My mom taught Tracy, Trisha, and me kindness and exemplified how important it is to care about others. No one worked harder than our mom to provide for us, and no one enjoyed spending time with her family more than she did. We couldn't save her from Alzheimer's but I know she is proud of all of us, our spouses, her grandchildren, and siblings for the way we kept her safe and cared for her when she needed us the most.

Todd Shimkus >

Todd Shimkus has been the President of the Saratoga County Chamber of Commerce since 2010, and his chamber career spans nearly three decades. He has a Master's Degree from Tufts University and a Bachelor's Degree from Clark University, both in Massachusetts. He lives in Saratoga Springs, New York, with his wife, Lisa. They have two adult children, Katelynne and Benjamin.

"I'm Not Ready for This" is Todd's first book, and he started to write it in September of 2020. The net proceeds from the sale of his memoir will be donated to the Amy's Army team in the annual Walk to End Alzheimer's to support caregivers and to find a cure for this disease. For more information, please visit **www.toddshimkus.com**.